Celebrity in Antiquity

CLASSICAL INTER/FACES

Series editors: Susanna Braund and Paul Cartledge

CELEBRITY IN ANTIQUITY

From Media Tarts to Tabloid Queens

Robert Garland

Duckworth

First published in 2006 by
Gerald Duckworth & Co. Ltd.
90-93 Cowcross Street, London EC1M 6BF
Tel: 020 7490 7300
Fax: 020 7490 0080
inquiries@duckworth-publishers.co.uk
www.ducknet.co.uk

A catalogue record for this book is available
from the British Library

ISBN 0 7156 3448 8
EAN 9780715634486

Typeset by Ray Davies
Printed and bound in Great Britain by
CPI Bath

Contents

There is only one thing in the world worse than being talked about, and that is not being talked about.

Oscar Wilde, *The Picture of Dorian Gray*

For Ling-Ling

Acknowledgements

My warm thanks to Susanna Braund and Paul Cartledge for inviting me to contribute to the Classical Inter/Faces series. Their encouragement at the beginning of the project and their exemplary attention to detail towards its end relieved me of many painful inaccuracies and deficiencies, linguistic as well as factual, and I could not have wished for better editors. What I resisted or simply failed to grasp is my sole responsibility.

The fact that I became engaged with this topic in the first place was largely thanks to Paul. His many talents include an attentiveness to the intellectual interests of his friends, who regularly receive newspaper clippings and articles relating to topics they are engaged with. Much came my way in this form while I was working on celebrity, and it provoked me to new ways of thinking. Contact with Paul by email is the best justification for succumbing to that medium that I can propose, and it sustains me in my fastness in Upstate New York. Like other books I've written, this one began as an article I wrote for *History Today*.

Introduction

We live in a global era of extremes: extreme media presence, extreme stories, extreme recognition. Everybody's out for some action – and those who succeed know how to stoke the flame .... Reality now is something to be created, played with, adjusted for maximum appeal .... With cable TV, the Internet, and the ballooning size of the media conglomerates, there is more need for content and airtime to fill. But what do we get? A lot less meaning and a lot less real product. Politics is often served up as scandal. News is more and more centered on the latest sensational drama. Stars edge out coverage of world events with breathless reports about their latest deals and endorsements. We get scoops on who is behaving badly with dizzy heiresses who sleep around, who dropped which agent, who wore what designer's dress and jewellery to transform himself into a human billboard on the red carpet. Call it a subliminal message about money, consumption, and a seemingly unattainable lifestyle. But the fact is, fame has come uncoupled from achievement and is an end in itself.

Maureen Orth, *The Importance of Being Famous:
Behind the Scenes of the Celebrity-Industrial
Complex* (New York 2004) 18

Celebrity status in the contemporary world is attainable by any jackass. Though talent, brains, energy, sex appeal, charisma and self-confidence still help, virtually anyone with a little ingenuity can pitch herself or himself into the forefront of the public gaze. I have only to chuck a condom of purple flour at the Prime Minister from the public gallery in the House of Commons to have my face plastered across the front page of every tabloid newspaper in the country. How difficult is that? Worse, with any tawdry little tale to tell I can be turned into one of those fly-by-night celebrities who populate cable TV. I won't of course remain in the spotlight for more than forty-eight hours. By then some other jackass will have taken my place. But that's the price we pay for the instant availability of this precious yet flimsy commodity. The fifteen minutes of fame famously identified by the attention-seeking Andy Warhol as everyone's birthright is the product of a technologically sophisticated age that has the means to shower celebrity status like confetti.

I want to be a celebrity!

To be famous simply for being oneself has become the ultimate aspiration. In response to the question 'What would you like to be?' in a questionnaire circulated around a Brooklyn high school a few years ago, two-thirds of the pupils replied, 'A celebrity.'[1] Though our modern celebrity culture has been at least a century in the making, the current intensity of its focus is a very recent phenomenon. When Elvis Presley died in 1977, he failed to make the cover of *Newsweek*. That distinction went instead to one Bert Lance, budget director for Jimmy Carter. Lance – this was the really hot news – had not been indicted by a grand jury. Compare the media's diffident handling of the King of Rock's death – potentially all the more sensational in light of his drug overdose – with the huge attention paid to ex-Beatle George Harrison's death by natural causes in 2001, to which *The Times* devoted its entire front page.

Again, when Marlon Brando died in July 2004, BBC World News chose to let this overshadow both the war in Iraq and events in the Gaza Strip. Editorial decisions of this sort speak volumes about society's values and priorities. And it isn't just the deaths of showbiz stars that grab the headlines. As the life and times of the attention-seeking Princess Diana proved, round-the-clock media attention can create an irresistible wave of public sympathy. Had Diana lived, there is no knowing where that wave might have borne her – nor what further damage it might have done to the British monarchy.

Never have we been so obsessed with the private lives of celebrities. We invade their privacy, imitate their style of dress, revel in their sexual indiscretions, and, if the chance arises, devour voraciously the sordid details of their downfall. The only area that still imposes the onus of role model is international sport, as the shaming of the two

Greek Olympic runners embroiled in a drug scandal at the Athens Games demonstrated: 'Just when the Olympic flame was being lit in front of the pre-eminent monument to mankind – the Acropolis, on the sacred rock which has illuminated human merit throughout the ages – a dark shadow begins to cross our screens', lamented the Greek newspaper *Eleftherotypia* (14 August 2004).

We also take immense pleasure in cutting our celebrities down to size. Just buy *Now* ('Your insight into the daily lives of the rich and famous') or *OK!* ('First For Celebrity News') or *People Magazine* or *Star* or *Glamour*, or simply log-on to gawper.com for the latest hot gossip. There's even a growing fashion for what is called 'celeb-trashing', in which a new breed of magazine and television show specializes. The aim is to catch the stars looking grotesque or fat – just like the rest of us most of the time. Conversely we pity celebrities for bearing the crippling burden of their celebrity. 'Come hear Jamie-Lyn Discala (an actress in the American HBO television hit series *The Sopranos*) share her surprising and inspirational story about overcoming the challenges of child stardom and the pressures of fame and perfection', gushed the poster for her public lecture at Colgate University in the USA.

Celebrity status has become an all-encompassing identity, irrespective of talent or vocation. When Ronald Reagan campaigned for the US presidency in 1980, pundits joked about his Hollywood background and claimed that his victory signified the triumph of style over substance. Twenty-four years later when Arnold Schwarzenegger stood for the governorship of California, those same jokes were effortlessly brushed aside. Schwarzenegger, of course, is a megastar, whereas Reagan was only a B-movie actor, but the change in the political climate was principally due to the fact that America had moved to a position of nigh absolute faith in celebrity, now seen as a valuable qualification for public office.

This said, it would be wrong to suggest that there was no precedent in modern times for the adulation that is now heaped upon celebrity. To name but two examples, both David Garrick (1717-79), the actor and theatre-manager, and later Lord Byron (1788-1824) became the object of sexual fantasies among their adoring fans. Even so, as Stefan Collini (2006, 476) pointed out in his analysis of the factors that have successively determined visibility in modern society: 'Roughly speaking, birth is the eighteenth-century principle, office the nineteenth, achievement the twentieth, and celebrity the twenty-first.'

Famous hero dies to become more famous!

The eponymous hero of *The Epic of Gilgamesh* is engrossed by the desire for immortal fame, which he erroneously conflates with immortality. The theme of the epic, as it has been reconstructed from fragmentary clay tablets that came to light in the library of the seventh-century BC Assyrian king Assurbanipal, seems to be to demonstrate the ultimate futility of such a quest. In the end Gilgamesh must accept that fame for fame's sake is self-destructive, especially when the search for it is uninformed by a proper sense of life's limitations.

A similar message pervades Homer's *Iliad*, whose central hero, like his Sumerian antecedent, is consumed with desire for imperishable glory (*kleos*). Glory is Achilles' *raison d'être*, much more so than the successful outcome of the Trojan War, which simply provides him with a field in which to exhibit his martial prowess to its fullest potential. He is afflicted, fatally one might say, with the culturally conditioned desire to receive his due desert. In a modern army he would be court-martialled, since he causes the deaths of countless fellow Greeks by going AWOL. The fact that no one accuses him of treasonable activity tells us much about Homeric society. Faced with a choice between living a long but undistinguished life and achieving imperishable glory but dying young, Achilles chooses the latter. In the *Odyssey*, when he is mulling over the meaning of existence in the company of the dead, he has an eternity to regret his decision: 'I'd rather be working for a dirt-poor farmer who barely scrapes a living than be lord of all the hosts of the dead,' he says ruefully to Odysseus, as the latter tries unsuccessfully to console him.[2] There's hardly a more sobering endorsement of life's primacy over fame in the entire western canon. In contrast to Achilles, Virgil's Aeneas, a hero of a very different stamp, is literally stopped in his tracks as he is about to court a 'beautiful death' and reminded of his familial obligations.[3] At the eleventh hour Aeneas comes to the important realization that we are here for others as well as for ourselves, and in so doing rejects the traditional heroic code.

The imperishable glory that Gilgamesh and Achilles seek is not at all, of course, the same thing as celebrity. Though the two obviously overlap, often as well they are in opposition. Each has its own trajectory and each, in different ways, is dependent upon changing tastes. Philosophers such as Cicero routinely rubbished celebrity on the grounds that all that it took for someone to acquire it was 'for a stupid and ignorant crowd to shout in unison'. Fame, on the other hand, being a more accurate measure of an individual's worth, was a more trustworthy guarantor of immortality.[4]

Latest research: Greeks didn't have a word for it!

Neither Greek nor Latin possesses a word that exactly conforms to the abstract English noun 'celebrity'. Greek approximations include *axiôma* ('estimation'), *charisma* ('magnetic appeal', commonly bestowed by a god), *doxa* ('repute'), *epiphaneia* ('renown'), *kleos* ('glory'), *lamprotês* ('distinction'), *philotimia* ('love of honour' or 'ambition') and *timê* ('honour'). Latin approximations include *claritas* ('renown'), *gloria* ('fame', especially that which results from military achievement), *laus* ('esteem', 'reputation') and *popularitas* ('popularity'). Other terms include *auctoritas*, 'authority' or 'ascendancy', a word which the Emperor Augustus virtually copyrighted and made exclusive to his position as First Citizen; *ambitio*, 'a striving for popularity', frequently through corrupt practices or excessive ostentation; *honos*, loosely translated 'honour', which primarily indicates the kind of distinction that comes with high office; and last but not least *celebritas*, our word 'celebrity', which, though it occasionally signifies 'the state of being celebrated', more frequently denotes 'a crowd' or 'commonness'.

Nor does either language have a word that exactly conforms to 'a person who is celebrated'. Greek adjectives include *endoxos* ('wellreputed'), *epiphanês* ('renowned') and *lampros* ('conspicuous'). Latin adjectives include *illustris* ('illustrious'), *clarus* ('famous', later restricted to men of senatorial rank), *famosus* ('famous', though more commonly used in the derogatory sense of 'infamous'), and *gloriosus* (occasionally 'illustrious', but more commonly 'vainglorious'). *Persona*, meaning 'a person of rank or social importance', hardly denotes a celebrity in our sense of the term.

'Celebrity', both as a state of being and as a person, is in fact a

5

relatively recent addition to the English language. The *Oxford English Dictionary* attributes the earliest usage to Dr Samuel Johnson, who peevishly complained (1751): 'I did not find myself yet enriched in proportion to my celebrity.' From early on a touch of superciliousness attached to the word, as in Matthew Arnold's observation (1863): 'Spinoza's successors had celebrity, Spinoza has fame' (note the telling variation in tenses). The first appearance of 'celebrity' to denote a person is attributed to the American poet and essayist Ralph Waldo Emerson, who spoke of 'the celebrities of wealth and fashion' (1848). The classic modern definition is that of the American historian and social commentator Daniel Boorstin (1961, 74), who tartly observed, 'Celebrities are known primarily for their well-knownness.'

Fan recognizes minor celebrity!

In light of all this, we might perhaps doubt whether either the Greeks or the Romans would have been familiar with the concept of celebrity and the kind of extroverted attention-seeking which frequently nurtures it. Plentiful evidence indicates that they were, however. Though a Gilgamesh or an Achilles or a Cicero would have despised 'mere' celebrity as something vastly inferior to the immortal fame they so earnestly craved, lesser mortals were less high and mighty, as this letter by the Younger Pliny[*] demonstrates:

> I have frequently received from the Senate as much fame (*fama*) as I could have wished, but I've never derived so much pleasure as I did recently from what Tacitus [the historian] said. He told me that at the recent chariot-races he had been sitting next to a Roman knight. After they had chatted about a number of learned subjects, the knight asked him whether he came from Italy or the provinces. Tacitus replied: 'You know of me from your reading.' Whereupon the man said: 'Are you Tacitus or Pliny?' I can't tell you what a source of joy it is to me to have our names bracketed together as if they belonged to literary works rather than to people, and to discover that both of us are known because of our

---

[*]For information about the sources quoted in this study, see Principal Sources (pp. 149-51 below).

work by people who would otherwise not have heard of us .... I have to tell you, I feel richly rewarded for what I've achieved.... And why shouldn't I take pleasure in the celebrity (*celebritas*) of my name?[5]

Pliny's delight at being identified as one of the leading luminaries of his day is exactly what a university professor, say, might experience today in similar circumstances, one whose name is recognized by only a few hundred persons in all. There is, after all, considerable gratification to be derived from being esteemed by people one has never met, even if it doesn't quite make one a celebrity. At the other end of the scale in the Roman world we encounter the megalomaniacal Emperor Nero, who stopped at nothing in his bid for a kind of popularity that came close to that of a contemporary pop idol.

With the exception of a few communal societies that look askance at attention-seekers, the phenomenon we are considering is probably universal. Certainly its importance within any given community should not be measured in numbers alone. Though there were relatively few Greeks or Romans who achieved widespread recognition of any kind, relatively few people do so in any age. Both Greek and Roman aristocrats adopted a variety of attention-seeking devices, and anyone of consequence was accompanied by a throng of supporters whenever he (much less commonly, she) appeared in public. The biographer Plutarch states that after Gnaeus Pompey had proved himself worthy of his bombastic title *Magnus* ('the Great') by being awarded a second triumph, 'he gradually absented himself from the Forum, appeared infrequently in public, and was invariably attended by a throng. You couldn't readily meet him or even see him without a mob. Rather he seemed to take pleasure in appearing with a large retinue ....'[6] In addition to politicians, other groups including philosophers, actors, charioteers, teachers, religious charismatics and physicians had their circles of devoted fans, who helped to win them recognition from the public at large.

Just as today, there were those who were motivated by what Dr Johnson in *The Vanity of Human Wishes* identified as 'the fever of renown', who would stop at nothing in their bid to become celebrities. Valerius Maximus, the early first-century AD author of a handbook entitled *Memorable Deeds and Sayings*, speaks of 'the cunning of those who in their desire for immortal fame did not scruple to gain notoriety even by crimes'.[7] One of the most pathological attention-seekers of all time was Herostratus, who set fire to the great temple of Artemis at Ephesus, one of the Seven Wonders of the ancient world, allegedly on the same night that Alexander the Great was born in 356 BC. When put to the torture, the arsonist confessed that he had been motivated by an insatiable appetite for celebrity.[8] The Ephesians executed him and made it a crime even to mention him by name, vainly hoping to deprive him of the posthumous fruits of his crime. Evidently it proved too good a story to expunge from the collective memory.[9]

The assassin of Philip II of Macedon was, we are told, similarly motivated. Pausanias, who was a member of Philip's bodyguard, is said to have asked his teacher, a sophist named Hermocrates, what he could do to become 'like a god among men (*epiphanestatos*)'. 'By killing the man who has accomplished the most', Hermocrates incautiously replied.[10] And so he did. Though the anecdote has all the signs of being apocryphal, it speaks of a culture that was fully cognizant both of the attraction of celebrity and of the pathology that it sometimes inspires. Similarly in the Roman world the Epicurean philosopher and poet Lucretius spoke contemptuously of the man who is 'consumed with envy when he sees with his own eyes someone who is powerful, someone whom everyone gazes upon, someone who struts his stuff'. Such a person, Lucretius goes on to say, 'wears himself out in pursuit of statues and a famous name'.[11]

*

A number of factors help to shape and define the scope of celebrity and its impact upon society:

Geographical context. Information is disseminated much more rapidly in a city, where there is a high density of population, than in scattered villages or townships, where there is a much lower density. Similarly in communities where travel is restricted reputations tend to be limited in scope. Important factors relating to the diachronic study of celebrity in antiquity therefore are the spread of communication in the Hellenistic world, and the increase in urbanization in the Roman world.

Arenas of communication. Some social contexts facilitate the attainment of celebrity. In the Greek world these include the symposium, the public assembly, the law courts, the festival games and the theatre. In the Roman world the imperial court, the theatre, the circus and the amphitheatre provided important contexts. Though these settings vary hugely in size, from merely a handful of individuals in the case of a symposium to as many as a quarter of a million in the case of the Circus Maximus, all are places where celebrity is on display.

Social status. Until recent times celebrity has always been most easily attained by those of royal or aristocratic birth, not only because such persons are naturally endowed with a high profile, but also because they possess the economic means to elevate that profile yet higher. The same was true in the Graeco-Roman world. Apart from those who belonged to the upper ranks of society, it was entertainers and professionals who had the best chance of attaining celebrity.

Access to the means of disseminating information. Though word of mouth has always been one of the most effective methods of spreading celebrity, other communicative means were employed by those with the necessary economic resources, such as commissioned literature, portraiture, and grandiose building programmes.

Strategic self-presentation. How and with what originality a would-be celebrity presents herself or himself to the public at large plays a vital part in the shaping of that person's public image. The tactics of strategic self-presentation include diction, style of dress and idiosyncratic mannerisms. A conscious awareness of this facet of celebrity is revealed in the famous last words of the Emperor Augustus – 'Have I played my part creditably enough in the theatre of life (*mimus vitae*)?'[12] – which are indicative of thé disjunction between the self and the social persona that any life lived in the glare of public attention entails.

Superficial though celebrity may seem as a topic of investigation, it provides an invaluable guide to the accomplishments and characteristics that a society most values and admires among its members, to its means of disseminating information, to the understanding of crowd psychology on the part of its most ambitious individuals, to the use and exploitation of public spectacle, and to the evolving geo-politi-

9

cal realities that over the course of time nurture the efforts of atten-tion-seekers.

At the same time I am fully aware of the limitations of data. Pliny apart, we have no first-hand testimony either from the celebrities themselves (telling us what it was like to be a celebrity) or from their adoring fans (telling us what it was like to be in their presence or confiding their fantasies to us). We know very little about the inner nature of our celebrities and are hardly in a position to determine to what extent they were motivated by, say, narcissism. We are unable to determine how heavily they relied on what sociologists today call nonverbal communication (body language, etc.) as a way of influencing their audiences and subjects. Was Alcibiades, for instance, a man of 'infectious optimism'? Did Alexander the Great have a 'sunny disposi-tion'? Was Julius Caesar possessed of 'a self-deprecating sense of humour'? Did the Emperor Augustus 'make people feel good about themselves'? Was the Emperor Nero 'always quick with a joke'? – all qualities incidentally that were attributed to Ronald Reagan. No treatise has come down to us from antiquity that investigates the power of personality. Arguably our best source is Plutarch, whose biographies of famous Romans and Greeks reveal a profound aware-ness of how strategic self-presentation facilitated the construction of a social persona or mask in antiquity.[13]

Consistent with the aims of the Classical Inter/Faces series, this study is necessarily brief. I have selected for investigation only a fraction of the highly accomplished attention-seekers of the ancient world. The first four chapters are diachronic and focus predominantly on a single individual, the next five investigate what we might call vocational celebrity (sports, religion, entertainment, etc.), and the final chapter is devoted to Queen Cleopatra and the Empress Theo-dora. My emphasis throughout is upon the types of achievement that bestowed celebrity-status in antiquity, the mechanisms by which it was promulgated, and the public response that it provoked.

Each chapter concludes with a postscript entitled 'Afterlife', which outlines the posthumous fame of the celebrities discussed within it only as far as late antiquity. While many celebrities, especially ath-letes and entertainers, disappeared without trace once their working lives were over, the reputations of others were preserved for hundreds of years, though many underwent considerable transformation, sometimes with immediate effect upon their demise. An obvious and striking example in recent times is Princess Diana, whom the tabloid press transformed overnight from manipulative bimbo to sainted martyr in the aftermath of her death.

In deference to the perennial appeal of the unabashed ego, I have attempted to write in a style that would have provided Oscar Wilde's Lady Bracknell with suitably sensational reading matter on her celebrated train journey. Megalomaniacs notwithstanding, there is much to relish in a subject that is both graced and disgraced by such a colourful cast of characters.

1

The Media Tart

Politics is just show business for ugly people.
Jay Leno, American chat show host

The world of the Homeric poems is one where information travels freely from one society to the next, unaffected by the friction of language, distance or ethnicity. Knowledge of the Trojan War, for instance, was so widespread that report of it is said to have 'reached the broad heaven'.[1] Even the solitary, one-eyed Cyclopes speak perfect Greek, while the Phaeacians, who live at the edge of the civilized world, are visited by bards who keep them abreast of the news. The fame of distinguished warriors and accomplished athletes is disseminated extensively, even though there is nothing to suggest that they were treated as actual celebrities. This fond evocation of Bronze Age cultural homogeneity is, of course, very largely the product of the poetical imagination, though it does, with some fidelity, evoke the world in which Homer himself lived.

That world in its politically most evolved form consisted of fiercely independent and largely self-contained city-states. Of the scores of city-states that existed throughout the Mediterranean, barely twenty had citizen populations in excess of twenty thousand, while the majority were considerably smaller. (The city-planner Hippodamus of Miletus thought that the ideal city ought to have ten thousand adult male citizens, whereas Plato put the number at a mere five thousand and forty.) Within such communities the names, though not of course the faces, of the most aggressive attention-seekers would have been familiar to virtually every citizen. Thanks, moreover, to an elaborate nexus of ties between aristocratic families who were often separated from one another by vast distances, some individuals were able to build up reputations that transcended national boundaries.

Aristocrats on charm offensive!

Around the middle of the sixth century BC a leading aristocrat named Pisistratus, desirous of establishing a tyranny, pulled off a highly successful publicity stunt by dressing up a tall girl called Phye (her name actually means 'Growth') as the goddess Athena and riding into Athens in a chariot with her at his side.[2] Athena's apparent endorsement of his political ambitions invested Pisistratus with a kind of celebrity that helped him to consolidate his grip on power. Even after the blue-blooded aristocrat Cleisthenes had broken the stranglehold that the nobility held over Athenian politics in the final decade of the sixth century, leading aristocrats continued to jockey with one another for power and prestige. They were still able to dominate the political scene after Athens had become a participatory democracy in 462/1 BC because the citizen body remained captive to the charms of wealth and privilege, even though its institutions symbolized, in theory at least, an ideological rejection of precisely those charms.

Participatory democracy provided a stimulus for some highly innovative kinds of attention-seeking. Largely because of the absence of organized political parties, personality played an even larger part in the shaping of public policy than it does in modern western democracies. Visibility – the closest Greek word is *lamprotês* – became an essential ingredient in the attainment of political success, since the more people one knew, the greater one's political clout. We might even go so far as to state that the respect that came from public recognition was the principal motivating factor underlying all forms of aristocratic competitiveness. The Greek word that best embodies this concept is *philotimia*, 'love of honour'.[3]

As Plutarch's biographies indicate, every Athenian politician developed his own idiosyncratic style of attention-seeking. Typical methods included lavish gift-giving and bribery, sponsoring public displays, making donations to the state or dedications to the gods, erecting elaborate gravestones to commemorate one's deceased relatives, and adopting a distinctive manner of self-presentation, through, say, hairstyle or apparel. Aristocrats competed with one another whenever they stood up in the Assembly or Council. But they also competed in more localized contexts, including the symposium and the gymnasium. Attention-seeking was in fact a structural part of the democratic system, since it was the duty of wealthy Athenians to subsidize big ticket items on behalf of the state, including taking charge of a trireme or 'warship' for a year or mounting a dramatic production. These obligations, known as liturgies ('work for the people'), provided aristocrats with a context in which to outshine their rivals, while simultaneously channelling their competitive instincts in the direction of public service.

Though it certainly wasn't confined to Athens, the struggle for celebrity status was particularly keen in this community precisely because the stakes were so high.[4] One of the most successful attention-seekers in the early fifth century was the politician and general Themistocles, who persuaded his fellow-citizens to direct their energies and resources into building a fleet so as to counter the threat of a naval invasion from Persia. He adopted the tactic of memorizing the names of as many Athenians as he could, rather as Ronald Reagan used to soften up the press corps by calling them by their first names at conferences. Themistocles came close to establishing – literally – a cult of his own personality. When the Persians were on the point of invading Attica, he boldly proposed that an oracle recommending to the Athenians that they 'trust in their wooden walls' be interpreted as an allusion to the stout timbers of their newly built fleet, rather than, in a more literal sense, to the wooden palisade surrounding the Acropolis. His advice prevailed, and the Athenians, along with a contingent of other Greek states, won a resounding victory in the straits of Salamis (480 BC). Themistocles subsequently established a cult in honour of Artemis Aristoboule ('Of the first-rate advice') because, in his presumptuous phrasing, 'he had given first-rate advice to the Athenians and Greeks'.[5] The cult constituted a veritable shrine to *amour propre* – a characteristic of celebrities throughout the ages.

Themistocles' younger contemporary Cimon, who was one of the major forces behind the establishment of Athens' maritime confederacy, hit upon the novel device of removing the fences around his property, so that, according to Plutarch, 'strangers and needy citizens' could avail themselves freely of his produce. He also provided meals for the poor, ostensibly so that they could fulfil their obligations to the state without the distraction of having to work for a living. Cimon would parade around Athens in the company of a cadre of smartly-dressed, handsome young men. Whenever he came across an elderly, down-at-heel citizen, he would instruct one of the young men to exchange garments with him. His generosity thus 'restored the legendary age of Cronos when wealth was liberally shared by all' – and his celebrity presumably skyrocketed accordingly.[6] Though Plutarch rejects the suggestion that Cimon adopted these tactics to curry favour with the common people, that, of course, was precisely the effect which his headline-grabbing tactics would have achieved. His biggest publicity stunt, however, was his recovery from the island of Skyros of the bones of Athens' legendary founder Theseus, which he repatriated 'with great pomp and ceremony'.[7]

The fifth-century politician who perhaps did least to court celebrity status was Pericles. He is said to have mesmerized the Assembly by his dignified manner, lofty style of speech, and extraordinary self-control. He hardly ever laughed, moved with grace, arranged his mantle with care, and spoke with control even when under stress. He rarely appeared in public outside the political arena and addressed the Assembly only on matters of the gravest importance. But though Pericles eschewed vulgar forms of attention-seeking, we needn't doubt that his cultivated aloofness was itself attention-grabbing.

By contrast Nicias, one of Athens' foremost generals during the Peloponnesian War, went so far as to engage the services of a publicity manager called Hieron to help him cultivate the image of a hard-working and self-sacrificing public servant. It was Hieron who, in Plutarch's words, 'helped him most to act out this part, by investing him with an air of solemnity and importance', notably by circulating stories about Nicias' rigorous work schedule and modest lifestyle.[8]

Interestingly, no Athenian of this period was honoured with a portrait in a public place. The one possible exception is Themistocles, a likeness of whom may have been displayed in the sanctuary of Artemis Aristoboule. Though the likeness has survived only in a Roman copy, the suggestion that Themistocles was responsible for commissioning the original fits well with the character of a man who in Plutarch's phrase was 'carried away by his desire for fame'. Since, however, Themistocles himself financed the sanctuary, it was perhaps not 'public' in the generally accepted sense of the term.

It wasn't until the beginning of the fourth century BC that it became acceptable in Greek society to erect an honorific statue during the subject's lifetime. Four examples are attested for the Athenian admiral Conon (at Athens, Erythrae, Ephesus, and on the island of Samos), and three for the Spartan navarch Lysander (at Delphi, Ephesus, and on Samos).[9]

'The Just' unjustly exiled!

The fact that the names of prominent Athenian politicians were far more recognizable than their faces is neatly exemplified by an anecdote relating to Aristides, one of the architects of Athens' maritime confederacy. Because of his reputation for absolute uprightness, Aristides was popularly nicknamed 'the Just'. Later in his career, however, when he was facing the threat of being ostracized from Athens for ten years, an illiterate country bumpkin, failing to recognize the great man, asked him if he would inscribe his potsherd with Aristides' name. (The word 'ostracism' derives from the potsherds or *ostraka* on which the votes at an *ostrakismos* were recorded. The politician scoring the most votes was exiled for ten years.) When the latter asked him whether this Aristides had done him any harm, the bumpkin replied 'No. It's just that I'm tired of hearing him called "the Just".'[10] Aristides thus fell victim to what we would call today celebrity over-exposure – a career hazard that overtook other prominent politicians, including Themistocles and Cimon, both of whom were also ostracized.

Comeback kid personifies democracy!

Celebrity is an amalgam of talent, lifestyle, charisma and sex appeal. The Athenian who scored highest in all these categories was Alcibiades. Alcibiades differed from most other politicians of this period, however, in that he sought visibility not to advance a particular political agenda – he seems not to have had one – but simply for its own sake. The fact that he was so successful is testimony to his larger-than-life personality. In many ways he personified Athenian democracy, since his chequered career exemplified the fickleness of the mob. His Roman biographer Nepos observed, 'The people thought there was nothing he could not accomplish.'[11] Plutarch wrote, 'It was impossible for anyone of any disposition to resist or be oblivious to Alcibiades, such was the charisma that he demonstrated in his daily

17

life and in his conversation, so that even those who feared him or were jealous of him succumbed to the charm of his company and presence.'[12]

What mattered most to Alcibiades were his own advantage and advancement. Nowhere was this more starkly demonstrated than in the debate about the feasibility of sending an expedition to Sicily. Rather than address the practical objections to the expedition raised by his opponent Nicias, Alcibiades, who strongly favoured the enterprise, interpreted the latter's opposition as a personal attack on himself, and he made his defence against that personal attack his main justification for going to war.

Alcibiades' career followed the now familiar path of the celebrity who rides high on the wave of public adulation at the beginning of his career, and then later, virtually overnight, falls from grace. But he was also the original 'comeback kid', capable of recovering more than once from the stigma of public ignominy. Like many of his kind, he enjoyed a love-hate relationship with the public. As the god Dionysus aptly observes in Aristophanes' *Frogs*, produced in 405 BC just one year before Alcibiades' death, 'The city longs for him and hates him and wishes to have him.'[13]

Fat old philosopher rebuffs drop-dead gorgeous poster boy!

Alcibiades was also the greatest poster boy that Greece ever produced. In fact he was one of the few personalities in the ancient world whose sex appeal is known to have contributed appreciably to his celebrity. Though his long-suffering wife Hipparete claimed that he mainly consorted with *hetaerae* (or courtesans), there can be little doubt that he was the number one heart-throb both for men and women, though whether his libido was in overdrive is unrecorded. It was rumoured that he had intercourse with his sister, his mother, his illegitimate daughter, as well as with a queen of Sparta. If Plato is to be believed, one person who did rebuff his sexual advances was Socrates, as Alcibiades admits self-deprecatingly in the *Symposium*. Since, however, Socrates prided himself on his sexual continence, Alcibiades could hardly have faced a stiffer challenge, so to speak. True or not, the report of a sex idol being given the cold shoulder by a fat old philosopher probably did wonders for the latter's posthumous reputation for self-control.

1. The Media Tart

Alcibiades was also an inveterate trend-setter. He refused to learn the flute on the grounds that the pursing of the lips was unbecoming to the bearing of a gentleman. (As a result flute-playing was dropped from the curriculum.) He cultivated a new style of sandal that others copied, dubbing them 'Alcibiades'. He had a lisp, which may or may not have been an affectation. He set a fashion for drinking in the morning. He dressed effeminately in a long purple cloak which trailed down to his ankles. Reputable Athenians regarded this practice with loathing – and their tongues no doubt wagged accordingly. It's difficult to appreciate how such a trivial aberration as the length of one's cloak could have caused offence, but we have to put the story in the context of a society that looked askance at the least manifestation of anything *outré*.

Alcibiades courted further controversy by decorating his shield with the unwarlike device of Eros, the personification of love, shown wielding a thunderbolt. This was presumably intended as a witty and irreverent counterpart to the usual assortment of gorgons, lions, bulls and boars favoured by the majority of Athenians. But it was also a way of taunting his critics by flinging in their faces the same charge of licentiousness that they brought against him.

Baddest man in Athens on rampage again!

Alcibiades lived life in the fast lane – in more ways than one. On one occasion he entered seven chariots at the Olympic Games and won first, second and either third or fourth prize. This was the most prestigious Olympic event, as well as the most costly to enter (see p. 72 below). He was one of the first individuals in history whose private life became the object of obsessive fascination. When he cut the tail off a dog for which he had paid the princely sum of seventy minas,* his friends told him that all Athens was scandalized. He merely laughed and said, 'That's exactly what I wanted. It'll stop them saying worse things about me.'[14]

His reputation for unruliness merely added to his celebrity. He attacked his school-teacher for failing to have a copy of Homer on him. He slew one of his slaves with a single blow of his staff. He thrashed a fellow-competitor who was financing a chorus. He locked his house-

*See Coinage, p. 155.

painter inside his house till he had finished the work. He struck his future father-in-law Hipponicus merely because he was dared to do so. It caused an uproar throughout the city. True to character, Alcibiades went round to Hipponicus' house next day and apologized. With a typically dramatic flourish he removed his cloak to expose his back and asked the victim to scourge him. The two men were publicly reconciled, probably in the presence of a large number of Alcibiades' supporters and hangers-on. Some years later when his wife Hipparete brought a divorce suit against him, Alcibiades seized hold of her in court and dragged her home through the streets. Such was his personal magnetism that no one dared lift a finger against him. The anecdote tells us a great deal about the extraordinary freedom that an aristocratic celebrity enjoyed in democratic Athens.

Disgraced politician undergoes extreme makeover!

Alcibiades had a 'portfolio identity', to adopt a term that was coined by management gurus in the 1990s to describe someone who markets himself as a collection of skills. Such individuals demonstrate little allegiance to any ideology or set of values. Instead they tailor themselves to the needs of the moment. As Plutarch observed, 'Alcibiades was endowed with one overriding characteristic which he used in his pursuit of people, namely that of assimilating himself to the behaviour patterns and lifestyles of others, so that he could change himself more radically than a chameleon.'[15] It was his capability of achieving extreme make-over – a characteristic which, *mutatis mutandis*, he shared with his cultural descendant Madonna – that enabled him to play the Athenians off against the Spartans during the Peloponnesian War.

Soon after being appointed one of the commanders of the naval expedition to Sicily in 415 BC, Alcibiades was accused of religious improprieties and summoned back to Athens to stand trial. He decamped to Sparta where he began collaborating with the enemy. True to his portfolio identity, he proceeded to out-Spartan the Spartans by 'letting his hair grow long, taking cold baths, eating coarse bread, and supping on black broth'.[16] His seduction of the wife of one of the two Spartan kings surely redounded to his credit by fostering the belief that his powers of attraction were well-nigh irresistible. It may also

20

have helped to rehabilitate him in the eyes of his countrymen, thereby paving the way for his eventual recall. The justification for his shameless action was characteristically self-serving: he claimed that he had impregnated Queen Timaea 'to ensure that his descendants would one day rule over the Spartans'. Since 'Alcibiades' was originally a Spartan name which entered Athens as the result of ties based on ritualized friendship between Athenian and Spartan aristocrats, he was also in a sense 'repatriating' it.[17]

In 413 BC he departed for Asia Minor where he took refuge with a Persian satrap and affected the Persian lifestyle. Some eighteen months later he helped secure a number of victories for Athens when the city was on the brink of defeat. As Plutarch perceptively noted, 'He now began yearning to see his home again, but even more to be seen by his fellow-citizens, since he had conquered their enemies so many times.'[18] He returned home in 407 BC to a hero's welcome – or, more precisely, to the type of welcome that is today generally reserved for a pop idol. His first public act following his acquittal from the charges lodged against him was characteristically headline-grabbing: he conducted the annual procession to Eleusis, home of the Eleusinian Mysteries, by land. (For the past six years security considerations had required initiates to be conveyed by ship.) It was, however, to be the last time that he would bask in his glory. Before the year was out he was held responsible for a naval fiasco and promptly relieved of his command.

Celebrity meltdown?

Alcibiades retired to the Thracian Chersonese (what we call today the Gallipoli peninsula), where he lived the life of a warlord. He later emerged from exile to warn the Athenians of the folly of beaching their ships on an exposed shoreline at a place called Aegospotami. His advice met with a rebuff, and the Spartans captured all but eight of their fleet, in effect winning the Peloponnesian War. Even at this late juncture, however, the Athenians continued to derive some comfort from the belief that their cause was not doomed so long as their number one celebrity remained alive.

Shortly afterwards Alcibiades was murdered, probably on the orders of a Persian satrap, with whom he had taken refuge. It seems he had been hoping to stage one last dramatic come-back by striking a deal with the Great King of Persia. It would be fascinating to know how he faced up to the realization that his stock of public goodwill had finally evaporated. Did he experience something akin to celebrity meltdown? As Maureen Orth has noted, 'The scorch of fame can be brutal, but the chill of the aftermath is an even stronger, more bitter sensation.'[19]

For all the frivolity and flamboyance that stamped Alcibiades' career, it is impossible to tell the story of late fifth-century Athens without assigning him a pre-eminent place. It is hardly an exaggeration to state that had he put his country first, Athens might not have lost the war. It tells us much about the character of its democracy that his fellow-citizens, no less than their enemies, proved so vulnerable to his charisma and that they took political decisions, often to their own detriment, accordingly. Even 'charisma' hardly does full justice to the force of his personality, for, as Thucydides wrote, 'Most people became frightened at the sheer scale of his lawlessness and sensual self-indulgence.'[20]

Alcibiades was the forerunner of the modern media tart – the attention-seeker who will go to any lengths to propel himself into the public eye, irrespective of the consequences for those around him. He was also one of the first celebrities in history to use his high profile to subvert traditional values. A born rebel, he scandalized his elders by thumbing his nose at the accepted norms of social behaviour, often for no better reason than to raise a storm. In many ways his life provides the textbook model of how to achieve celebrity in an age unfamiliar with the means of mass communication, and for better or worse its modern manifestation owes much to his trail-blazing example.

Spartan general worshipped as a god!

Had the Athenians taken Alcibiades' advice at Aegospotami, there is a faint possibility that the tide of war might have turned in their favour. There is an even fainter possibility that they might have established a cult in his honour. Instead, the distinction of becoming the first Greek to receive divine honours during his lifetime went to the Spartan admiral Lysander, coincidentally the victor at Aegospotami. The initiative seems to have been taken by oligarchs on Samos, who were deeply grateful to him for restoring them to power at the end of the Peloponnesian War. They renamed their games in honour of Hera 'Lysandreia', and cities throughout Ionia instituted sacrifices in his name. It's worth noting that Lysander, like Alcibiades, had the kind of personality that revelled in celebrity, and he may well have done much to court this unprecedented honour. He is said to have employed a poet called Choerilus of Samos, who composed impromptu verses in his honour.

A new idea was in the air, and it would gather pace in the coming decades. The vainglorious Clearchus of Heraclea (a Greek city on the south-west shore of the Black Sea) began dressing like Zeus and named one of his sons 'Thunderbolt', after Zeus' most common attribute. Philip II of Macedon, as we shall see in the next chapter, sought to put himself on a par with the gods – thereby fuelling the ambitions of his emulous son Alexander.[21] To conclude, the cult of personality had come a long way in the course of the fifth century BC: when Miltiades, who had been largely responsible for the Athenian victory over the Persians at Marathon (490 BC), requested a simple crown of olive as a token of his achievement before the Assembly, one of his detractors angrily replied, 'When you have beaten the barbarians in single combat, Miltiades, then you may demand to be honoured separately.'[22]

Afterlife

The reputation of Themistocles as one of Athens' most gifted politicians and generals increased appreciably after his death and he ultimately came to outshine all his rivals, including Pericles. One of his greatest admirers was Thucydides, who commended Themistocles for his extraordinary foresight in equipping Athens with a navy in anticipation of the Persian invasion. The Greek travel-writer Pausanias reports seeing a statue of him in the Prytaneum, the symbolic centre of Athens and arguably its most prestigious civic space.[23] In Roman times he assumed the stature of Winston Churchill: Cicero, for instance, said that 'by leading his fellow-countrymen in the Persian Wars he had saved them from slavery'.[24] A century and a half later Plutarch, defending Themistocles against what he saw as a downplaying of his achievements by the historian Herodotus, described him as 'the man most directly responsible for saving Greece'. He further stated: 'If there are Antipodeans living beneath the earth, I don't imagine that even they have failed to hear of Themistocles.'[25]

Themistocles' head appeared on the reverse of Roman coins that celebrated Athens' victories in the Persian wars.[26] His fall from grace and subsequent exile served as an object-lesson in the ingratitude of the mob and it made him the obvious counterpart to the Roman general Coriolanus, who was also rejected by his countrymen. He was buried in the agora of the Greek city Magnesia in what is today central Turkey – an extraordinary honour that was granted only to truly exceptional individuals in antiquity – and his tomb was venerated throughout antiquity. The Magnesians also bestowed honours upon his descendants for more than half a millennium after his death.[27]

Alcibiades' genius for stirring up controversy ensured his immortality. A speech entitled *Against Alcibiades* is preserved within the corpus of speeches by his contemporary Andocides. Though it alludes to events around the time of the Sicilian Expedition, it is thought to be a rhetorical exercise of later date. Plato in the *Gorgias* exonerated Alcibiades from all blame for Athens' downfall, holding his predecessors, Themistocles, Cimon and Pericles, responsible instead.[28] The debate continued into the Roman period. Nepos states, 'It is agreed by all who have written a life of him that no one exceeded him in either vice or virtue'.[29] Valerius Maximus confessed that his mind was torn 'between execration of the man and admiration'.[30] In the eyes of the satirist Persius he exemplified the archetypal rake who exploits his noble ancestry, good looks and rhetorical know-how to work the mob up into a passionate frenzy.[31]

Perhaps in part because he was antithetically paired with Socrates in Plato's *Symposium*, Alcibiades' name became a byword for debauchery, decadence and demagoguery. Several portraits of him, none extant, are attested in Roman times. A statue was set up in the *comitium* (or place of assembly) in the Roman Forum around the middle of the fourth century BC – to the surprise of Pliny the Elder, who thought that the honour should have gone to Themistocles.[32] The Emperor Hadrian, who could certainly lay claim to being an aficionado of male beauty, was so enthralled by Alcibiades' legendary good looks that he erected a marble statue in his honour and sacrificed an ox to it annually.[33]

The Royal Icon

All the time I feel I must justify my existence.

Prince Charles

Alexander the Great, who became king of Macedon at the age of twenty, is arguably the most charismatic figure that the ancient world produced. Such was his celebrity that there is a doubtful report that the Romans, who had very little contact with the Greeks in this period, dispatched an embassy to his court. A variety of grandiose goals have been attributed to him. It is alleged that he was eager to spread Greek culture throughout his conquered territories, that he aimed to fuse the Greeks and the Persians into a single race, that he was inspired by the dream of fostering universal brotherhood, or, more mundanely, that he craved world domination. His empire ultimately stretched from the Adriatic in the west to the Punjab in the east, and from Afghanistan in the north to Ethiopia in the south. Since the only mechanism for holding the empire together was Alexander himself, it was inevitable that his personality should occupy centre-stage. As the leader of a Panhellenic enterprise whose objective was to conquer the barbarians, moreover, he faced a major image-crisis in that a large number of Greeks considered the Macedonians to be semi-barbarian. To overcome their deep-seated prejudice, he sought to market himself as a thoroughgoing Greek.

Alexander's own relationship with his public persona is, however, impossible to fathom, due primarily to the mystical nature of his personality, and though he may have derived some satisfaction from his celebrity, we do not know this for a fact, as he was anything but a conventional self-promoter. He certainly wasn't interested in fame for fame's sake. Though Plutarch repeatedly refers to his *philotimia* ('love of honour') and *philoneikia* ('love of rivalry'), he also noted, 'It was not every kind of glory that he sought, and he did not seek it in every kind of action' – unlike his father Philip II, who, for instance, minted coins which alluded to his victory in the horse-race at the Olympic Games.[1] To some extent Alexander was spared the need to promote himself by virtue of his royal status, though it should be noted that Macedonian kingship was hardly comparable to a modern monarchy. It was a much more informal institution, with the king interacting almost exclusively with the warrior class. We know very little about how his subjects perceived Alexander. We don't even know for a fact whether they took special pride in his accomplishments.

What makes Alexander so difficult to read is that he seems to have been convinced by his own propaganda, to the extent that we should perhaps not label it propaganda at all. He is therefore one of the most fascinating and most elusive attention-seekers of all time, who interpreted the concept of image primarily in symbolic terms and whose ascent to stardom followed an internal logic of its own. Though he became a household name, his face would not have been recognizable to the majority of his subjects. In fact what makes Alexander virtually unique among our celebrities is that he chose to circumscribe the terms in which he could be classified as such. Yet the fact remains that by the time of his death his celebrity was greater than that of anyone ever before him. He had reigned for just twelve and a half years.

Barbarian 'descended from Zeus'!

Whereas aristocrats and tyrants had played by the rules in their bid for attention, Alexander's father Philip II, who ultimately acquired domination over the entire Greek mainland, effectively tore up the rule-book. In 346 BC he had made his mark at Delphi by celebrating the Pythian Games under his presidency. In 338, in celebration of his victory over the Athenians and the Thebans at the battle of Chaeronea, Philip began building a monument that became known as the Philippeion near the west wall of the Altis or sacred enclosure of Olympian Zeus at Olympia. In it he displayed statues of himself, his parents, his wife Olympias, and his son Alexander. While 'officially' proclaiming himself to be the champion of the panhellenic ideal, Philip was brazenly boasting that Macedon's royal house was Greece's first family. The statues were made of gold and ivory over a wooden core – a highly suggestive choice of materials, since chryselephantine statues had previously been erected only to the gods. So by bestowing quasi-divine status on himself and his family, Philip was in effect elevating their personalities to an unprecedented level of visibility. Since, moreover, Olympia was the greatest of the panhellenic sanctuaries, his action would have enjoyed maximum exposure. It also had the incidental benefit of enabling him to remind the Greek world at large that the Argead dynasty to which he belonged had an impeccable pedigree, as it was descended from Heracles, the son of Zeus. Being circular in structure, moreover, the Philippeion resembled a hero shrine, though whether Philip received heroic honours in it during his lifetime is uncertain.[2]

City named after Macedonian youth!

The erection of a family shrine at Olympia was not the only act of hubris that Philip perpetrated. Early in his career he had renamed a rich mining town 'Philippi' (modern Philippi in north-east Greece). He also gave his name to Philippopolis (modern Plovdiv in Bulgaria). This precedent was followed by his son, who at the age of sixteen named a town in Thrace 'Alexandroupolis'.[3] Philip was away on a military campaign at the time. It would be fascinating to know how he reacted to the news on his return. All that we know for certain is that the name stuck.

In the course of his career Alexander established a large number of new foundations, both cities and military outposts, which he liberally endowed with his name, though Plutarch's claim that he founded over seventy is almost certainly a wild exaggeration.[4] But even if he founded only six, as a recent, highly conservative estimate has proposed, these six, given their geographical locations, would have promoted his visibility in parts of the world that had previously been entirely ignorant of Greek culture, including Baluchistan, Pakistan, Tajikistan and Afghanistan.[5] His first and greatest foundation was Alexandria in Egypt, situated in the western Delta near the mouth of the Nile, which by the first century AD had an estimated population of three hundred thousand. The most distant was Alexandria Eschate ('The Farthest'), which was over four and a half thousand miles from the Macedonian capital. Its remoteness speaks volumes about the reach of his reputation.

Boy wonder is 'born-again Achilles'!

Like every educated Greek, Alexander was steeped in the verses of Homer. Legend has it that he kept a copy of the *Iliad* under his pillow at night. One of his most brilliant ploys – but was it propaganda or did he actually believe it? – was to market his campaign against Persia as a re-run of the Trojan War. On several occasions during his career he also pointedly re-enacted ('acted out' might be a better phrase) episodes from the Trojan War so as to underscore the heroic and epic nature of his undertaking.

His primary role model was Achilles, the bravest of the Greek warriors, from whom he claimed descent on his mother's side. As soon as he set foot in Asia, Alexander performed a sacrifice at Achilles' supposed tomb outside Troy. Then again, before he faced the Persian king Darius at the River Issus, he sacrificed to Thetis, Nereus, the Nereids and Poseidon, just as Achilles does before his duel with Hector in *Iliad* XXII. When his close friend Hephaestion died, Alexander's inconsolable grief was such that it invited comparison with the grief of Achilles at the death of his friend Patroclus in *Iliad* XVIII. Other mythological exemplars helped him to construct an identity that seamlessly blended the legendary with the here-and-now. The famous story of his taming a wild stallion called Bucephalas in his youth may have been modelled on the story of the infant Heracles wrestling with two snakes. His march across the desert to the oasis at Siwah (see below) may in part have been a bid to rival the heroes Heracles and Perseus, both of whom were said to have visited this region.[6]

We'll never know to what extent Alexander saw himself as the reincarnation of Achilles and to what extent he was merely play-acting. His unique sense of selfhood led to a blurring of the boundaries between his own identity and his chosen role models, and this in turn helped to validate the purpose and legitimacy of his Asiatic campaign. How his army responded to his evocation of the past defies investigation. Nor do we know what impact it had upon the Persians. But however improbable it may seem to us, we need to bear in mind that the values of the heroic world continued to resonate powerfully in a socially and politically backward state like Macedonia. It may well be that the famed exploits of these ancient heroes, as reinterpreted by Alexander, served to inspire the young, and that part of his motivation

28

was to present himself to his peers as a role model whose accomplishments equalled those of the legendary greats.

Beards are out - the chin is in!

Alexander employed portraiture so successfully in the crafting of his public image that he effectively converted himself into an icon. To this day his personality remains so bound up with that image that it is virtually impossible to tell the two apart. To assist him in this aim, he commissioned 'official' portraits from the leading artists of the day – the bronze sculptor Lysippus, the painter Apelles, and the gem engraver Pyrgoteles. He may in fact have been the first Greek ever to sit for a portrait. There is even a report that he issued an edict forbidding anyone else to make a portrait of himself, though this claim was probably inspired by the example of the Emperor Augustus, who sought to control imperial portraiture (see p. 57 below).

Though numerous portraits of Alexander have come down to us, most are believed to have been produced after his death.[7] No original bronze has survived, though a number of Roman copies are thought to have been inspired by Lysippus' composition. A characteristic feature of the portrait-type is Alexander's beardlessness, which distinguishes him both from his father and from all his contemporaries. In a society where appearance and presentation were so uniform, this in itself must have created quite a stir. In the long term it started a trend, making shaving fashionable throughout the classical world. Beardlessness was in fact adopted by all the Hellenistic kings who succeeded Alexander, as well as by the Roman emperors. The first emperor to break with the trend was Hadrian in the early second century AD. Beards then became obligatory until the reign of Constantine, which saw the return of the clean-shaven look.

The fad for beardlessness thus constitutes an early instance of celebrity look-a-like syndrome, since anyone with a razor could model himself upon the most powerful man in the world. Other characteristic features of Alexander's portrait-type include the deep-set eyes and distant gaze, the mane of thick, flowing hair tossed back from the forehead with its characteristic off-centre parting that is suggestive of heroic, almost godlike energy, and the tilting of the neck slightly to the left. All these features are evident in the so-called Azara herm dated *c.* 330 BC, arguably the most famous contemporary depiction of Alexander to have survived. (The bust takes its name from a Spanish ambassador named José Nicolas Azara, who presented it to Napoleon.)

We don't know how closely Alexander resembled his official portrait, but we should not assume that he was particularly handsome.[8] It's even conceivable that he commissioned it partly to present himself in a more flattering light. This would be consistent with the tradition that the Persian queen mother Sisygambis mistook him for his friend Hephaistion, who was allegedly 'taller and better-looking'. We also don't know whether Alexander directed where the statues should be displayed. Though there are numerous references to statues of Alexander in later literature, fewer than ten full-scale examples were to our knowledge commissioned by the king himself. So if, as Andrew Stewart (1993, 55) has surmised, Alexander's face ultimately became 'the most famous in history', this had relatively little to do with Alexander himself. And even if we add to these the portraits that were commissioned by members of his court, his flatterers, and cities seeking to curry favour with him, the total number documented for his lifetime is still well under a hundred, especially if we omit the minor arts from our count. Admittedly this exceeds the number of likenesses of any Greek before him – a mere six are attested for his father – but the fact remains that Alexander's idealised features may well have been virtually unknown to the overwhelming majority of his subjects, including the Macedonians themselves.

Scholars are undecided about whether Alexander used coinage to disseminate his image among his subjects. Certainly there was a precedent. Nearly a century earlier Lycian dynasts subject to the Persians had begun issuing coins with heads that were probably intended to be self-portraits on the obverse. However, the only securely identified depiction datable to Alexander's lifetime appears on two coin-types that were probably minted in India during his campaign against a local king called Porus.[9] As Alexander is represented full-length in both 'portraits', however, they do not suggest even an approximate likeness. (They also happen to be the only full-length images of Alexander that can be dated to his lifetime.) They were probably struck not by him but by one of his officers, perhaps in commemoration of a victory.[10]

2. The Royal Icon

Alexander preferred to decorate his coinage with images of gods and heroes. Zeus, Ammon, Dionysus and Heracles were his particular favourites. He did this to claim their endorsement of his political ambitions, in much the same way that his successors would mint coins with his head on them to claim his endorsement of *their* political ambitions (p. 35 below). Alexander's association with divine and heroic personages also served to symbolize his immortality as the founder of an empire – certainly a more grandiose ideal than that of promoting a cheap cult of personality. It is also conceivable that he refrained from publicizing his image in the belief that this would detract from the mystical aura in which he sought to envelop himself.

Spin doctor in tailspin!

Shortly before departing on his Asiatic campaign, Alexander commissioned a pupil and nephew of Aristotle named Callisthenes of Olynthus to accompany him on his travels and write an official history of his campaign. Little is known about how Callisthenes went about fulfilling his brief, but he must have been admitted into Alexander's most intimate circle. He may even have gained access to his official papers and been allowed to consult Alexander's officers. In effect Callisthenes became the world's first embedded reporter, though whether he periodically sent instalments of his work back to Greece in the style of his modern counterpart is not known.

Alexander's employment of Callisthenes was a blatant attempt to alter the historical facts to his own advantage. Although the *Praxeis Alexandrou* or *Exploits of Alexander* survives in only a handful of fragments, we know that it was distinctly eulogistic in tone, not least because it defended Alexander's claim to be descended from Zeus. It was primarily targeted at non-Macedonian Greeks, whose political support Alexander was keen to enlist. As an early exercise in military propaganda, however, it was a complete failure. Later writers wrote scathingly of its sycophantic and sensational tone, and it is hardly likely that contemporary readers were disposed to be more generous. Callisthenes was summarily executed in 327 BC for allegedly plotting against Alexander's life and for refusing to perform obeisance (see p. 33 below). Though the details of his downfall are unclear, it is not inconceivable that the charge of treason was trumped up by members of Alexander's inner circle, who were jealous of his presence in their midst.

Callisthenes wasn't the only writer who, so to speak, came along for the ride. Alexander also engaged an epic poet called Choerilus of Iasus (coincidentally the same name as the encomiastic poet hired by Lysander) to sing his praises in hexameter verse. Though he rewarded Choerilus handsomely for his efforts, those efforts, in the collective verdict of antiquity, resulted in poetry of irremediably mediocre quality.[11]

Suicidal desert march!

The most puzzling incident in Alexander's entire career was his decision to visit the oracle of the god Ammon at Siwah in the Libyan desert in the spring of 331 BC. From a military point of view the march served no function whatsoever. It might well have proved disastrous, since it provided King Darius with an opportunity to launch a counteroffensive at a time when the logical move for Alexander was to follow up on his recent victory. Rarely has any general undertaken such a strategically purposeless military exercise in the middle of a campaign, and it raises serious questions, to put it mildly, about Alexander's sense of priorities. The second-century AD historian Arrian ascribes three motives to him: to consult the oracle, to rival the achievement of his ancestors Perseus and Heracles, and to trace his descent – or perhaps his conception – back to the god Ammon. Very possibly Alexander justified the expedition on all these grounds. The fact that his troops followed him, apparently without demur, is powerful testimony to their unwavering investment in his compelling sense of selfhood.[12]

History does not record what question Alexander put to the oracle when he arrived at Siwah nor what answer he received. Once again, the mystery surrounding the encounter probably increased public interest in it. It was, however, widely reported that the oracle addressed him as the son of Ammon. Shortly afterwards other oracles followed Siwah's lead, including that of Apollo at Branchidae on the modern Turkish coast.

Though the desert march seems on the surface to have been little more than a perilous distraction from the serious business of winning the war, the report of it must have greatly enhanced Alexander's reputation by enabling him to consolidate the belief that he was of divine ancestry. Its military purposelessness in fact may have been exactly commensurate with the degree of wonder that it aroused.

Macedonian makes Greeks grovel!

Alexander's father at least toyed with the idea of receiving divine honours. On the occasion of the marriage of his daughter Cleopatra, Philip ordered a statue of himself 'worthy of a god', as the historian Diodorus reports, to be carried into the theatre behind those of the twelve Olympian deities, evidently to suggest that he was equal to the twelve and like them worthy of receiving worship.[13] This act of hubris must have outraged the crowd, which included guests from all over the Greek world. Their outrage was, however, very short-lived, as the king was assassinated by one of his bodyguards just minutes later (see p. 8 above).

Whether Philip would have officially demanded divine honours from the Greeks if he had lived is unclear. His son, however, did. The visit to the oracle of Ammon seems to have been an important step along the route towards what Paul Cartledge (2005, 245f.) has identified as deification by degrees. The Egyptian priesthood had already hailed him a god, as they did every Pharaoh, and he may also have received heroic honours as the founder of Alexandria.

The culminating moment occurred at Bactra (modern Balkh in southern Afghanistan) in the winter of 328-327 BC, when Alexander demanded *proskunêsis,* technically the gesture of blowing a kiss, from his Greek and Macedonian courtiers. In Persian eyes *proskunêsis,* which was sometimes accompanied by a bow or complete prostration, merely signified deference to a social superior. From a Greek perspective, however, it was understood as an act of worship performed exclusively before a god. Very likely Alexander sought to capitalize on its ambiguous significance. By demanding obeisance from his courtiers he might have hoped to avoid the embarrassment and odium of explicitly claming divine honours, though in effect this was what it implied.[14] Deification was, after all, the only remaining step upwards for a celebrity of his unprecedented status.

Afterlife

Alexander's posthumous reputation merits a separate study in itself, and all I offer here are a few highlights. His corpse had hardly been washed when an argument flared up over who should succeed him. No one did, as he had failed to put into place a mechanism by which his successor could be chosen. But the fact that he died young with his life's task (whatever it may have been) uncompleted greatly intensified the magnetic appeal of his personality for future ages. The so-called Parian Marble (inscribed 264-263 BC), an epigraphical record of the most famous dates in Greek history, uniquely describes his death as a 'transformation'. Oddly, we do not know at what date, on whose initiative, or in what circumstances Alexander was first accorded the title 'Great'. The earliest surviving mention occurs in Plautus' play *Mostellaria*, dated *c.* 200 BC. It was also at an unknown date that his birth came to be attributed to miraculous conception, demonstrating that he had possessed divine powers.[15]

Nothing illustrates more emphatically the potency of Alexander's reputation at the moment of his death than the fact that his former general Ptolemy, several years before declaring himself Ptolemy I Soter king of Egypt, kidnapped Alexander's body while it was en route from Babylon to the royal vault in Macedonia, in order to further his dynastic aims. In fact it was largely because he projected himself as the official guardian of Alexander's mortal remains that Ptolemy was able to claim superiority over the other successors to his empire. After a brief sojourn in Memphis, the mummified corpse was transferred to Alexandria, where it was encased in a glass sarcophagus and placed inside a magnificent tomb. It remained on display for well over five hundred years. Its ultimate fate is not known. The tomb became the focus of a cult of Alexander as a 'founder god', first of Alexandria and later of the Ptolemaic dynasty itself. Partly because of the tie to Alexander, the city became the cultural capital of the Hellenistic world, though its future prosperity owed most to its natural advantages, which included excellent harbours and access to the interior of Egypt.

Some time after 311 BC, a Greek cult of Alexander began to spread throughout Egypt. In 279 BC, to demonstrate his seniority among the other Hellenistic kings and also to celebrate the close link between

Alexander and the Ptolemaic dynasty, Ptolemy I's son, Ptolemy II Philadelphus (see p. 122 below), staged a magnificent festival known as the Ptolemaieia, to which he invited delegates from all over Greece and the eastern Mediterranean. The festival was revived every four years and did much to boost the prestige of the Ptolemies. A cult of Alexander was also established by the Seleucid dynasty in Syria to rival the Ptolemaic one, as well as in many parts of Greece. Both in Egypt and in Syria, Alexander's birthday was celebrated as a national holiday.[16]

Posthumous portraits of Alexander were produced in a variety of media. Both in order to lay claim to his legacy and to legitimize their own authority, his successors minted coins with his head on the obverse. No fewer than ten different Alexander-types are known. The earliest were struck by Lysimachus in Thrace and by Ptolemy I in Egypt in *c.* 300 BC. A variety of attributes adorn the head, including the horns of Ammon, the scalp of the Nemean lion slain by Heracles, an elephant scalp (an allusion to Alexander's victories in India), and a royal diadem. In Macedon, by contrast, where there seems to have been some aversion to capitalizing upon his achievements, coins continued to display the head of Heracles on the obverse. Numerous free-standing statues of Alexander were erected in Hellenistic and Imperial times. It is even possible that Alexander's features were reproduced on the face of the Colossus of Rhodes, one of the Seven Wonders of the Ancient World, which was erected on Rhodes in *c.* 305 BC. Particularly celebrated today is the 'Alexander Mosaic', which was found in the House of the Faun at Pompeii. This is thought to be a Roman copy of a Greek original by Philoxenus of Eretria. Though it celebrates Alexander's victory over Darius at the battle of Issus, the artist's sympathy seems to lie not with the youthful Macedonian but with his ageing opponent.

Pyrrhus, king of Epirus, who took on the Romans in south Italy in the 280s BC, liked to think of himself as a latter-day Alexander the Great. He was in fact distantly related to the Macedonian and had equally big dreams, his being to build a vast empire in the west, just as Alexander had done in the east. Pompey, hailed 'the Great' at twenty-three by his troops, very deliberately modelled himself on Alexander, even affecting a similar hairstyle, though less leonine. Alexander's afterlife was also fostered by the Emperor Augustus, who

likewise sought to compare himself with the greatest military commander that the Greek world produced. When he visited Alexander's
tomb in Alexandria after his victory at Actium, he placed a garland on
the deceased's head and strewed the body with flowers. On being
asked if he wished to visit the tombs of the Ptolemies, he pointedly
replied: 'I came to see a king, not a row of corpses.'[17] In a further act
of apparent homage, Augustus exhibited two paintings of Alexander
by Apelles in the most prominent part of the new forum that he built
in Rome.[18] He also reproduced Alexander's tousled hair in his sculptural portraits, as, too, did his grandsons. However, his involvement
with his idol remained quite superficial, for one could hardly conceive
of two more different and distinct personalities. If therefore Augustus
could not hope to emulate him (lacking as he did the least aptitude for
war), the next best thing was to suggest, albeit somewhat nebulously,
an emotional kinship with the warrior-leader's achievements.

Framed by his incomparable achievement and his romantically
early death, Alexander's life, more than that of any other figure from
antiquity, offered itself up as a suitable subject for myth-making. Fact
and fiction eventually coalesced into a fantastical narrative known as
the *Alexander Romance*, to give the work its generic title, which is
based only very loosely on the historical facts. The narrative was first
put together in the third century BC in Alexandria, though certain
elements are thought to be much older. A definitive version took shape
around the beginning of the first century AD, again in Alexandria. It
remained hugely popular into the Middle Ages and beyond, and was
translated into some thirty-five languages.

The earliest Roman biography of Alexander is by Cornelius Nepos,
who included it in a lost work entitled 'Kings of Foreign Races'. Livy
deliberated at length as to how the Roman Republic would have fared
in a war with Alexander.[19] (He patriotically concluded that the Romans would have won hands down, even if confronted with 'a
thousand armies more formidable than those of Alexander and his
Macedonians'.) Alexander's exploits were well-known to Pliny the
Elder, who frequently cites them in his *Natural History*. Plutarch
pairs Alexander with Julius Caesar in his collection of *Parallel Lives*.
He also wrote an essay entitled *On Alexander the Great's Good Fortune or Good Qualities*. Appian's obituary of Caesar takes the form of
an extensive analysis of the characteristics and accomplishments that

the two men had in common.[20] Quintus Curtius Rufus, author of the only surviving history of Alexander in Latin, mixes criticism of his divine aspirations with encomium.

In philosophical circles, Alexander's reputation was rather mixed. Some saw his murder of Callisthenes as a blight upon his career. Seneca the Younger described it as 'the everlasting crime of Alexander, which no amount of courage, no success in war, will redeem.' He added, 'Whenever anyone says, "He conquered everything as far as the Ocean and even attacked the Ocean itself with ships that were unfamiliar to those waters and extended his empire from a corner of Thrace to the boundaries of the East", it will be said, "But he killed Callisthenes. Although he exceeded all the achievements of generals and kings in antiquity, none of what he did will be as great as this crime." '[21] By contrast, Aulus Gellius, the Roman miscellanist, commended him for his continence, as demonstrated by his refusal to set eyes on Darius' wife, celebrated for her beauty, after he had taken her prisoner, for fear that he would be tempted to ravish her.[22]

3

The Consummate Populist

I have only one valuable possession, it is held in my heart, it burns in my soul, it abides in my flesh and aches in my nerves: it is the love that my people have for me.

Eva Perón, wife of Argentinian President
Juan Perón and idol of the poor

It would not be far-fetched to interpret Julius Caesar's entire career as a very public bid to satisfy his giant-sized ego. Certainly it could hardly be claimed that he unswervingly put the good of Rome first. He was, however, a creature of his age, in which the attainment of power depended to a preponderant degree on self-publicity. Other leading politicians such as Sulla and Pompey were interested as much in their public standing as in what they could do for Rome, and their egos feasted on the adulation of the military and the urban mob alike. The fact that Sulla was honoured with the title '*Felix*' (Blessed; Fortunate) and Pompey with '*Magnus*' (Great) tells us much about the giant shadows that such men cast as they strutted their stuff across the public stage.

In the first century BC the welfare of the Roman Republic had increasingly come to depend upon the talent and energies of a handful of outstanding individuals, who, in line with its expansion, came to arrogate to themselves ever more power and whose political rivalries contributed decisively to its breakdown. On the one hand, legionaries became increasingly reliant upon the generals under whom they served, both for cash disbursements and for land allotments upon their retirement. On the other hand, members of the urban plebs, desirous of welfare and entertainment, formed deep attachments to their high-profile benefactors, of whom Julius Caesar was a spectacular example. Though their attachment proved unreliable in the months leading up to his assassination, it produced such an outpouring of grief at his funeral that it affected the whole course of Roman history.

The emergence of an urban mass in the first century BC has profound implications for our topic of investigation. It is estimated that Rome's population in this period was between half and three-quarters of a million, and other cities were growing at a comparable rate. Henceforth urbanization would play an increasingly important part in the history of celebrity. Rome had become the celebrity capital of the ancient world, followed by Alexandria in Egypt, Seleucia in Iraq, and Antioch in Syria.

Giant egos in deadly competition!

Caesar tried to cloak his preoccupation with his ego by terming it '*dignitas*', a word roughly corresponding to 'public standing'. In many ways, however, he was the most egregious offender. As he publicly acknowledged, and evidently without fear of censure, it was in large measure to preserve his precious *dignitas* that he initiated the Civil War between himself and Pompey the Great. Though this attribute was essential to every élite Roman's self-image, Caesar's *dignitas*, having been conferred on him by the Republic, was, in his own words, 'dearer than life itself'.[1]

We learn much about the extraordinary power of personality in the Late Republic from the fact that wounded *dignitas* could be advanced as a legitimate justification for initiating a war that ultimately came to envelop almost the entire Roman Empire. Resulting as this did in the deaths of hundreds of thousands of Romans, as well as the forced dislocation of perhaps as many more, it was the culminating act in a drama of competitiveness that had been intensifying for well over half a century. It also represented the ultimate bid for public attention on the part of two playground bullies, each of whose primary political objective was the elimination of his rival.

It was not, however, the over-sized egos of the Late Republic who first discovered the benefits of thrusting themselves into the public eye. Rivalry and factiousness had existed from the earliest days of the Republic, as, too, had awareness of the dangers they posed. The constitution had been founded on the principle that no single individual should achieve lasting domination, and there were structural checks and balances to prevent precisely such a situation from arising. It was the stresses and strains resulting from Rome's expanding

Empire that ultimately caused the system to break down, and it is through the impact of Caesar's charismatic personality that we can see the fault lines exposed most clearly.

Hostage threatens captors!

While en route to Rhodes in his early twenties, Caesar was captured by pirates.[2] The incident presented him with his first opportunity to grab the headlines. After a considerable sum of money had been paid for his release, he circulated the story that he had bullied his captors into raising the ransom they had originally been demanding by a factor of twenty-five. He had even (or so he alleged) threatened to crucify them if they released him – a threat he eventually carried out.

The picture of a Roman youth demonstrating such total contempt for his captors would have scored a big hit back in Rome. Since the only surviving witness to the conversation was Caesar himself, however, it is not improbable that he invented it. He certainly knew how to sex up his reputation when the situation demanded. In 49 BC, when he was taking the momentous step of crossing the River Rubicon and initiating the Civil War, he claimed that he saw 'an apparition of wondrous stature and beauty, who sat and played on a reed' – presumably the god Pan – urging him forward.[3] Caesar was by no means the first Roman to indulge in self-mythologizing. While laying siege to Carthago Nova (modern Cartagena in Spain) in 209 BC during the war against Hannibal, Publius Cornelius Scipio Africanus announced to his troops that the god Neptune had appeared to him in a dream, promising aid.[4]

Virtual unknown elected!

Caesar's patronage of the urban plebs would today be labelled conservative populism. Although the meetings and assemblies at which Roman magistrates were elected and bills passed into law were still dominated by the propertied classes, from the final decades of the second century BC the plebs had become a political force in their own right, as we see from the fact that aspiring politicians were allying themselves to their cause. Even if only a small percentage of their number turned up at an assembly, this could still determine the outcome of a vote, since a belligerent crowd can be extremely menacing.[5]

Caesar passed numerous laws to improve the lot of the poor, such as founding new settlements and mandating that large landholders include at least one-third of freemen in their workforce, instead of relying entirely on slaves. But he also resorted to more eye-catching tactics as well, including hosting public banquets, handing out generous allowances of grain, and, last but by no means least, sponsoring spectacular entertainments, such as plays, wild beast hunts, athletic competitions, and gladiatorial contests. Before he appeared on the scene, gladiatorial contests had largely been confined to aristocratic funerals, the belief being that the shedding of blood could appease the spirits of the dead. Thanks to his initiative, they were now increasingly mounted primarily for the delectation of the masses.

Caesar first sponsored a gladiatorial contest to mark the twentieth anniversary of his father's death when he was standing for office as one of the two curule aediles, junior magistrates who were responsible for the orderly running of Rome. Three hundred and twenty pairs of gladiators, decked out in silver armour, fought to the death in the Forum, the most high-profile space in the capital. By claiming that the contest was being held in honour of his father, Caesar maintained the fiction that he was presiding over a traditional act of devotion to the dead. The controversy generated by this semantic parsing no doubt contributed to his renown. He became an overnight celebrity – surely one of the first in history.

Twenty years later Caesar crowned his quadruple triumph (see below) with a series of games entitled the *ludi Victoriae Caesaris* or 'Games in honour of Caesar's victories', which were celebrated over a period of about ten days. He was now, however, Dictator for Life and no one could raise any objection. In the future, aspiring politicians would follow his lead in order to further their ambitions. Under the Principate emperors regularly hosted games to enhance their popularity, a spectacular example being those sponsored by the Emperor Trajan (see p. 114 below).

Pontiff supreme in fashion!

The Romans observed a very strict dress code, which made their group-affiliation instantly identifiable. On public occasions ordinary citizens wore a plain white toga, knights one with a thin purple stripe, and senators a toga with a broad purple stripe. So strictly did they adhere to this code that Valerius Maximus even devoted a small section to 'Those distinguished men who indulged themselves in clothing or other features of style more freely than ancestral custom permitted'.[6] The fact that Valerius could come up with only three examples from the whole of Roman history indicates how conservative his countrymen were.

Caesar stood out from his fellow-citizens by virtue of the fact that as *pontifex maximus* or Supreme Pontiff, Rome's senior religious official, he wore a richly embroidered toga decorated with red and purple stripes, thought to have been modelled on the attire once worn by the kings. He further drew attention to himself by what we would call today creative accessorizing. He wore a loose fitting belt and sported flashy rings. Like many celebrities, he sought to disguise his baldness, in his case by wearing a laurel wreath on all public occasions, an honour that was granted him by the Senate. If Serengeti sunglasses and hair plugs had been available, Caesar would, I suspect, have invested in them.

The eagles have landed!

Caesar's most enduring military accomplishment was the conquest of Gaul. This not only increased the size of the Roman Empire by approximately a quarter, but also gave it a wholly different character, since it was now no longer focused exclusively on the Mediterranean. There were, however, deep-seated problems with the campaign. In the first place the conquest was undertaken without the approval of the Senate. Secondly, Caesar's extended command came perilously close to being illegal. And thirdly, he committed some serious military blunders, notably by invading Britain – an extremely ill-fated exercise, which placed his entire campaign in jeopardy.

In order to counter the hostility and suspicion of the Senate, and perhaps as well to appeal to the plebs over its head, Caesar devised the innovative strategy of publishing military dispatches entitled *Commentaries on the Gallic War*, which provided a narrative of the campaign seen from the front line and through the eyes of its commander-in-chief. In so doing, he was following the lead of the Dictator Sulla, who had written up his memoirs in twenty-two books. Though essentially accurate in outline, Caesar's *Commentaries* are an artful blend of *suggestio falsi* (suggestion of falsehood) and *suppressio veri* (suppression of the truth), which enabled the author to impose his version of events on Rome's reading public. (A modern analogy is Winston Churchill's *A History of the Second World War*, which also engages in a degree of special pleading.) In particular, Caesar exculpates himself from any charge of waging an aggressive war against the Gauls. Instead he casts himself in the role of the model provincial governor – cautious, far-sighted and shrewd, intervening only at the behest of Rome's allies and invariably with an eye to Rome's national security. He rarely mention his legates, gives them little credit for his success, and, so far as he ever admits to a major setback, invariably ascribes it to the capriciousness of the goddess Fortuna.

The *Commentaries* are written in a plain and direct style and they use a very limited vocabulary (some 1,300 words in all). These factors guaranteed their popular appeal. Though we have no idea how many copies were produced, it is likely that within the limits of ancient 'book' production they constituted one of the world's first best-sellers. Their effectiveness as propaganda was greatly enhanced by Caesar's use of the third person – a brilliant literary device which distances the author not only from the events he is describing but also from the persona he is seeking to create. Though we do not know what impact the *Commentaries* had in the formation of public opinion, the fact that Caesar wrote a sequel when he waged war against Pompey suggests that they were indeed highly effective. They also served the no less important function of keeping Caesar in people's minds during his extended absence from Rome.

Dictator's quadruple triumph!

Celebrity status among the élite was most closely identified with military glory, the highest attainment of which was the award of a triumph. A triumph was, indisputably, the greatest show on earth. It was the Roman equivalent to winning an Oscar for best actor, best director and best screenplay all in the same year, with the important stipulation that five thousand extras, namely the enemy, had to have been killed in a single engagement.

The whole of Rome turned out to witness a triumph, jamming the streets along the route. Dressed in a purple toga emblazoned with stars, the *triumphator* drove down it in a chariot drawn by four white horses. In his left hand he bore an ivory sceptre mounted by an eagle, symbolizing victory in war. Accompanying him was a procession made up of captives and veterans, as well as senators and magistrates. After threading its way through Rome, it entered the Forum and proceeded to the foot of the Capitoline Hill. At this point the *triumphator* dismounted from his chariot and climbed on foot to pay tribute to Rome's foremost deity, Jupiter Optimus Maximus (Best and Greatest), whose temple was located on its summit. It must have required a steady head to keep a sense of human limitations in the face of the tumultuous roar of the crowd. For good reason, therefore, a slave rode beside the *triumphator*, holding a laurel wreath over his head and repeatedly pronouncing, 'Remember you are mortal', while his veterans chanted scurrilous verses of the kind one reads today on lavatory walls.

Pompey the Great had been awarded three triumphs. Caesar trumped him by racking up four – in part by 'triumphing' over his fellow citizens. Caesar's quadruple triumph, which he celebrated in September 45 BC, was in many ways the high point of his career. It was also the most lavish public spectacle ever mounted in the capital. Each triumph was 'themed', a brilliant innovation for which Caesar himself must be given full credit: citrus wood for the Gallic triumph, tortoiseshell for the Egyptian triumph, acanthus wood for the Black Sea triumph, and polished silver for the Spanish triumph. By its conclusion tens, if not hundreds of thousands of Romans had set eyes on Caesar's face, which for good measure he had painted with vermilion dye to resemble the face of the celebrated statue of Jupiter Capitolinus housed on the Capitoline Hill. It is hardly surprising that the Roman triumph later provided the template for the Nazi rally.

Victor is victim of edifice complex!

Since architecture is partly about power, it's hardly surprising that Rome's greatest generals sought to immortalize their military successes by erecting monuments financed from the spoils of their wars. To commemorate his triple triumph in 61 BC, for instance, Pompey had built an elaborate architectural complex in the Campus Martius or Field of Mars, north of the Capitoline Hill. It included a huge portico in the form of a rectangular precinct, a theatre – the first permanent structure of its kind to be erected in Rome – and a temple to Venus Victrix (Conqueror). In case anyone missed the point, a statue of Pompey was erected either inside the theatre or in the portico, surrounded by images of the fourteen nations he had subjugated.[7]

Armed with the enormous wealth derived from his Gallic campaign, Caesar again upstaged Pompey by building a new forum on the north-east flank of the Capitoline Hill. This, the so-called Julian Forum, was planned as an annex to the original Forum, which lay a short distance to the south. As well as glorifying Caesar's military achievement, the project created goodwill by providing long-term employment for the poor. The purchase of the land alone, which required the expropriation of a commercial district, set him back a cool one hundred million sesterces.[8]

Even when we compare it with the grandiose imperial *fora* that were built after it, the Julian Forum was massive in scale (160 by 75 metres). Pliny the Elder went so far as to compare it with the pyramids of Egypt. The centrepiece was an all-marble temple to Venus Genetrix (Mother), which stood on a podium five metres high. As the Julian *gens* or clan to which Caesar belonged claimed descent from Venus, the temple in effect proclaimed his divine ancestry, though to quiet his critics he could always claim that the goddess in question was the mother of Aeneas, founder of the Roman race. The choice of the epithet 'Genetrix' was a further way of thumbing his nose at Pompey, since it suggested a more intimate relationship with the goddess than the latter's epithet 'Victrix'.

Dictator shoulder to shoulder with kings!

The right to erect a statue of oneself in a public place was still controlled by the Senate in Caesar's day, as it had been from the early days of the Republic. The first politician to be granted such an honour was Lucius Minucius, who had rescued Rome from famine in the early fifth century BC. Over the course of time, however, many Romans had managed to circumvent the law by claiming that their statues were intended as votive offerings to the gods. One of the first was the Dictator Quintus Fabius Maximus Cunctator (Delayer), so named because of his policy of attrition in the Second Punic War, who set up a statue of himself on the Capitoline Hill. By 158 BC the Forum had become so cluttered with statues of magistrates that the censors were instructed to remove all except those that had been erected by resolution of the people or the Senate.[9]

It was therefore a mark of exceptional honour that the Senate decreed that several statues of Caesar should be erected in the capital.[10] There was one on the Capitoline Hill beside those of the seven kings of Rome, another in the Roman Forum, an equestrian statue in the Julian Forum, and, rather improbably, others 'in every temple in Rome' according to the historian Dio. Major Italian cities erected statues in his honour, as did cities in the Greek East. This development could hardly have taken place without at least Caesar's tacit approval. To overcome the instinctive Roman aversion to commemorative portraiture, he was commonly depicted standing beside either the goddess Roma or Victoria (Victory).

From the period of the Civil War onwards Caesar's likeness also began to appear on coins. Ever since the introduction of coinage, the moneyers responsible for making discs for stamping in either bronze, silver or gold had had the right to stamp the coins they issued with their own names. From the middle of the first century BC onwards they were entitled to depict their own (or someone else's) head on the obverse. The earliest known numismatic portrait appears on a bronze coin issued at Nicaea by Caius Vibius Pansa, who had served with Caesar in Gaul, in 48-47 BC. Shortly before his death Caesar was awarded the right to issue coins stamped with the words 'Parent (or Father) of the Fatherland', presumably beside his portrait. There is, however, nothing to suggest that he obtained or sought the right of exclusive portraiture on coinage, as Augustus did after establishing the Principate.

Dictator's PR gaffes!

In the final months of Caesar's life all eyes became increasingly focused upon him, as speculation about his long-term plans intensified. It is hardly surprising that the pressure finally got to him. He became indifferent to his public image and, worse, increasingly megalomaniac. The Senate's grovelling behaviour certainly didn't help matters. It heaped a series of fatuous honours upon him, including

Dictator for Life, Prefect of Morals, and, as noted above, Parent or Father of the Fatherland. The month *Quinctilis* was re-named *Julius* (July). Caesar was granted permission to sit on a gilded throne, to wear a triumphal robe, and to sport a laurel crown on all public occasions. His birthday was celebrated as a public holiday. An oath was taken to defend his laws and his person. Though he was not elevated to the rank of god, he was awarded divine honours – just one step below – and the consul Mark Antony was appointed as his priest. The year before his death bronze coins were issued depicting the thunderbolt, symbol of Jupiter, behind his head. (A statue of Caesar, clothed in the aegis and wielding the thunderbolt, was found in Constantinople.) Though grateful Greeks had occasionally bestowed divine honours upon Roman generals, this was the first time that one of their number had received this distinction from the Senate.

The final months of Caesar's life were marked by a series of public relations gaffes that seriously undermined his public image and alienated him from the populace. The first occurred at the Latin Festival, held in commemoration of the unification of Latium, when he gave a very public dressing-down to two tribunes of the plebs who had reprimanded someone for placing a diadem, the symbol of Persian and Hellenistic Greek royalty, on his statue in the Forum. The second was when he failed to rise as members of the Senate approached him with a copy of a decree listing the honours they had just awarded him. The third took place just a month before his death at the Lupercalia, a festival intended to promote fertility. On this occasion Caesar appeared in the traditional dress of a Roman king and was offered a diadem by Mark Antony. Though he repeatedly declined the diadem and conspicuously ordered that it be placed in the temple of Capitoline Jupiter, the incident further fuelled suspicions about his long-term ambitions. It was these gaffes which induced the sixty or so men who conspired to assassinate him to believe that his death would be greeted with universal rejoicing – totally erroneously as matters turned out.

Corpse grandstands at own funeral!

It is one of the supreme ironies of history that if Caesar had actively sought to ensure that he would go out in style he could hardly have done a better job than the assassins. There are few parallels for the wholly unprompted outpouring of grief that Caesar's funeral generated in any period of history, though those of Eva Perón and Princess Diana in recent times come close. While Mark Antony deserves a lot of credit for whipping up the crowd to fever point by removing Caesar's shroud and displaying his mangled body to the multitude of mourners, we can also detect the hand of the Consummate Populist assiduously at work behind the scenes.

As soon as the mourners learnt that Caesar had bequeathed his lavish gardens to the Roman people plus the sum of seventy-five *denarii* to each citizen, they tore up the temporary wooden benches placed around the Forum and cremated him there and then – an extraordinary and unique honour. It was arguably the most effective posthumous relations exercise ever mounted in history. Never before had Caesar been a bigger celebrity. Never before had a corpse spoken so eloquently at its own funeral.

Afterlife

Despite the spectacular nature of his death and the popular unrest that it generated, it was by no means a foregone conclusion that Caesar would achieve the status that he holds today as the most famous Roman who ever lived. This depended in large measure on the political aggrandizing of his grandnephew and adopted son Octavian, who began styling himself 'Caesar' some two weeks after Caesar's death. Following Caesar's deification on 1 January 42 BC – an action which, in the opinion of his biographer Suetonius, reflected the judgment of virtually all Romans – Octavian acquired the designation *divi filius* (son of the deified). In addition, he consecrated a temple to the deified Julius at the exact spot in the Forum where his body had been cremated. It is proof of the Dictator's enduring hold over the Roman imagination that the temple was repaired by the Emperor Hadrian in the early second century AD and that it survived into late antiquity.

Octavian's inclusion of the name 'Caesar' in his titulature (*Imperator Caesar divi filius Augustus*) was followed by all the Julio-Claudians. For the Flavians who succeeded them in AD 69 'Caesar' became the title of the emperor's designated successor. When the Emperor Diocletian established a tetrarchy at the beginning of the fourth century, the two junior partners both took the name. The title was finally abandoned in AD 360 at the end of the dynasty established by Constantine, though it was revived in the Byzantine world. Roman legions continued to celebrate the anniversary of Caesar's deification well into the Christian era, thereby preserving his reputation for affability among the rank and file of the soldiery.

The contemporary historian Sallust, a client and supporter of Caesar, gave his patron a prominent role in his account of the *Catilinarian Conspiracy* (written three years after Caesar's death), notably by attributing to him a speech in which he opposed on principled grounds the execution of a group of conspirators who had been arrested on the charge of seeking to ignite a revolution. In the century following his death, however, Caesar's reputation came to polarize public opinion, as it continues to do to this very day. His presence in Augustan poetry is distinctly muted. The obsequious court historian Velleius Paterculus, whose career spanned the reigns of both Augustus and Tiberius, was the first to compare him with Alexander the Great. The trope was later adopted by Plutarch, who paired the two generals together in his *Parallel Lives*. A century afterwards the historian Appian followed Plutarch's example.

Pliny the Elder identified Caesar as 'the supreme example of intellectual vigour', although he also claimed that he had killed 1,192,000 men in battle (not including his own fellow citizens in the Civil War!) – 'a mighty if unavoidable wrong inflicted on the human race', as he soberly reflected.[11] Lucan, a contemporary of the Emperor Nero and the author of an uncompleted epic poem about the Civil War, depicted Caesar as a bloodthirsty tyrant who single-handedly brought about the downfall of the Republic. The Emperor Nero (as was his wont) forced Lucan to commit suicide in AD 65 – perhaps in part because his poem was seen as an attack on the Judio-Claudian dynasty. Even so, Lucan's trashing of the founder of the dynasty may well have enjoyed support among a disenchanted intellectual élite who held Caesar responsible for the vices of his successors. In the early second century AD Suetonius' biography sought to do justice to his extraordinary personality, while also giving full credit to his military accomplishments. In his polemic entitled *Against the Pagans* (AD 417/8) the Christian apologist Orosius cites Caesar as the epitome of pagan arrogance.

A number of cities preserved Caesar's name, although primarily in deference to Augustus Caesar. They include Caesaraugusta in Spain (modern Zaragoza), Caesarea in Iran (modern Kasseri), and Caesarea Maritima in Judaea (modern Kaisaria), which Herod the Great converted from a Hellenistic fortress into a harbour in 22 BC and provided with all the amenities of a Roman-style town.

4

The Imperial Superstar

*Like all the best families, we have our share of eccentricities, of
impetuous and wayward youngsters and of family disagreements.*
                                                      Queen Elizabeth II

By the weight of his press clippings alone the Emperor Augustus
would have easily outdone any Roman before him. That is because the
Principate, as we call the system of government that he established,
channelled public attention undeviatingly towards the First Citizen or
princeps. It was a system that could best be comprehended through
the personality and accomplishments of one man. One of the chief
differences between it and the Republic which it claimed to restore but
effectively replaced was that the Principate removed the chaotic clam-
ouring for public attention that had characterized the preceding century. As an institutional model it would hardly change until the turn
of the fourth century AD when Diocletian went even further by elevating the emperor almost to the position of an oriental monarch – aloof,
despotic and untouchable.

What makes Augustus so fascinating from the perspective of this
investigation is the fact that, like Alexander the Great before him,
he was anything but a conventional attention-seeker. The status
that he attained in 27 BC was worlds removed from the high visibility that his great-uncle had courted so aggressively. Thanks to a
subtle form of interplay between him and the Senate, this status
greatly advanced his constitutional agenda. He now took the title
'Augustus', meaning 'Consecrated', 'Revered' or 'Worshipped', the
Greek equivalent of which was '*Sebastos*'. It was perhaps the nearest equivalent to 'Superstar'. Of course, it helped immeasurably
that his reign lasted more than forty years, since this enabled his
pre-eminence to become an accepted fact of political life. It also
helped that his right-hand man, Marcus Vipsanius Agrippa, a
highly accomplished military tactician who sponsored an ambitious

programme of public works in the capital, had no apparent desire to hog the limelight.

Acutely aware that Caesar's assassination had been prompted in part by the public objections to his acceptance of unprecedented honours, Augustus consistently sought to avoid the suspicion that there was anything constitutionally irregular about his role. On the surface the *auctoritas* ('authority') to which he laid claim was an expression of the uniqueness of his personality, though it was also through this same quality that he held the reins of power. His style of self-presentation was in many ways the exact opposite of that which is adopted by most celebrities today, and in this principally resided his incomparable genius for self-promotion. For though he could hardly prevent the gaze of his subjects from being permanently directed towards him, he was fully aware of the dangers of over-exposure. Accordingly he projected himself as the embodiment of the *mos maiorum*, the traditional code of behaviour sanctioned by the ancestors. And far from giving himself airs, he conversed easily with people of every social rank, showed deference towards the Senate, and lived very modestly.

But while cultivating the image of a public servant who was selflessly devoted to the common good, Augustus also ruthlessly eliminated all the outlets for self-advertisement that had previously been available to the inner circle of senatorial nobles under the Republic. He did this by downplaying the many contributions made by his henchmen and allies towards the peace and prosperity of Rome. Triumphs in particular became a rarity, as these presented the ultimate opportunity to upstage the emperor.[1] It is the tension between these two opposing tendencies – Augustus' studied rejection of the more vulgar forms of attention-seeking, on the one hand, and his exclusive control over all means of self-promotion, on the other – that makes the study of his superstar status so instructive.

Tomb tops skyline!

Like Pompey and Caesar, Augustus exploited architecture as an expression of his egotism. Probably a year or two before the final showdown between his forces and those of Mark Antony at Actium in 31 BC, he announced very publicly that he was the number one man in Rome by planning a colossal tomb in the Campus Martius. This building, known officially as the Mausoleum, invited comparison with the eponymous tomb and hero-shrine of the Carian ruler Mausolus which was regarded as one of the Seven Wonders of the World, though it may also have been inspired by the tomb of Alexander the Great in Alexandria.

Over eighty metres in diameter and nearly forty metres high, the tomb was surmounted by a cylinder upon which stood a colossal bronze statue of Augustus himself, estimated by some scholars to have been over seven metres tall. Intended as a family as well as a personal mausoleum, it openly proclaimed the dynastic ambitions that under-pinned the Augustan Principate. The first person to be buried in it was Augustus' much-loved nephew Marcellus, who died in 23 BC.

Augustus' Mausoleum greatly exceeded any previous structure of its kind in the capital and it would remain unsurpassed in size throughout antiquity. (Hadrian's tomb, built a century and a half later, which is known today as Castel San Angelo, would equal it but tactfully not surpass it.) He probably intended it to be read as a response to Mark Antony's leaked desire to be buried beside Cleopatra in Alexandria, for by announcing so emphatically his own decision to be buried in Rome, he was sending an important message about Rome's primacy. The fact remains, however, that the Mausoleum was also a crass piece of architectural propaganda, and it no doubt offended as many people as it impressed.

Other major building projects of this era that helped to raise Augustus' profile include the dedication of a spectacular temple of Apollo on the Palatine Hill. One of its porticoes housed a colossal bronze statue of the god whose features, it is said, bore a close resemblance to those of Augustus. Augustus also built a magnificent new forum in the area between the recently completed Julian Forum and the foot of the Viminal Hill. The crowning feature was a temple to Mars Ultor (Avenger), which he had vowed to the god before the battle of Philippi in 42 BC following the defeat of Caesar's assassins, and which he finally dedicated in 2 BC. Architecturally it bore a close resemblance to the temple of Venus Genetrix erected by Caesar; in scale it was one and a half times bigger.

Arena death toll record broken!

Like Caesar, Augustus sponsored lavish games at regular intervals throughout his reign. As Suetonius reports, 'He surpassed all his predecessors in the frequency, variety, and spendour of his games.'[2] One of his first public acts after accepting Caesar's legacy was to host an extravagant series to overshadow those that had been mounted a short time before by the assassin Marcus Brutus. In the course of his reign he sponsored eight gladiatorial games and twenty-six animal games. Later emperors followed his example, each in turn seeking to outdo his predecessor: in the first century AD the regular celebrations lasted 88 days, in the second century 135 days, and in the fourth century 176 days. Games were also held on an *ad hoc* basis, the most notable instance being the 123 days of celebrations which the Emperor Trajan sponsored in AD 107 to commemorate his victory over the Dacians.

As well as providing entertainment, games also afforded the plebs an opportunity to observe the emperor and his family, since they frequently appeared together in the imperial box. Suetonius reports that the plebs took particular pleasure in the fact that Augustus demonstrated the same passion for the games as themselves – unlike Julius Caesar, who made use of the occasion to catch up on his correspondence.

Augustus ensured that the most lavish entertainments were mounted either in his name or in that of his heirs. From 22 BC onwards he closed down the principal avenue for self-advertisement available to praetors (judicial magistrates one rank below consuls) by limiting the number of gladiators whom they could display on any given occasion to a hundred, while reserving for himself the right to sponsor shows that were more than ten times bigger. Four years later he restricted the right to celebrate a triumph to members of the imperial family. Henceforth non-family members would have to content themselves merely with the *ornamenta* (insignia) of a triumph.

The effusive tributes, technically known as *acclamationes*, which the emperor received from his grateful and adoring subjects whenever he hosted games can properly be interpreted as an expression of support and appreciation for the Principate itself, as personified by the First Citizen, whose superstar status they thus validated and confirmed. *Acclamationes* were also delivered at other events he attended, including festivals, public feasts, theatrical performances and circus races. Over time they became the chief communicative medium between the emperor and the Roman people.[3]

Images of chief everywhere!

Augustus' image, repeatedly reproduced in the capital and throughout the Empire, was itself a symbol of the Principate. Some two hundred and fifty or so sculpted portraits have survived, over eighty of them from Rome alone, and the original total would have been many times greater. They were paid for by an assortment of ambitious careerists and grateful provincials, all eager to establish their credentials as a 'friend of Caesar' or, more obliquely, as a 'friend of Rome', as the inscriptions upon them regularly state. Many of the statues derive from a likeness that was perhaps made by an unknown artist to commemorate Augustus' triple triumph in 29 BC. The likeness in question reflects Augustus' desire to present himself to his subjects as a model of affability and aloofness consistent with his title of 'First Citizen'.

While the majority of the portraits were probably busts, many were larger-than-life statues. The most famous surviving example is the Prima Porta, so-named after its find-spot in Rome. It depicts a barefoot, slightly larger than life-size Augustus in the pose of a Greek hero wearing ceremonial battle dress. (This was, incidentally, very different from Augustus' actual physical appearance – of below average height, with spots all over his body, decaying teeth, and troubled by an occasional limp.) The centre of the breast-plate shows a relief of a defeated barbarian returning a legionary standard to a Roman commander. This was a pointed allusion to the fact that Augustus had secured the return of the standards captured from Marcus Licinius Crassus by the Parthians in 53 BC. The reality, however, was somewhat different, in that Augustus had achieved this feat by diplomatic means alone.

The emperor's profile also began to dominate the coinage. The earliest examples date to the period of the so-called Second Triumvirate that followed the assassination of Julius Caesar. In the wake of his victory at Actium, a series was minted with his profile on the obverse, and Peace and Victory on the reverse. From 20 BC onwards Greek cities began placing the emperor's portrait on their coins. Given the quantity of coins in circulation in this period, the total number of images of Augustus in existence should be reckoned in the millions. So the inhabitants of the most distant parts of the Empire knew his face from the coins they used every day.

Very probably there was also a highly profitable market in crude reproductions of the emperor's features. Fronto, who kept up a regular correspondence with Marcus Aurelius in the late second century AD, observed that poorly executed pictures of his patron could be found 'on moneychangers' tables, in stalls, in shops, hanging in the eaves, in entrance halls, in windows – in fact everywhere'.[4]

Poets praise Principate!

Augustus enlisted the services of leading poets in the hope that they would agree to write flattering panegyrics in his honour. Though he didn't quite get what he bargained for, he did at least receive a measured endorsement for his vision of a return to traditional values. One of the best examples is the *Carmen Saeculare* or Secular Hymn, which Horace composed to mark the birth of the new *saeculum*. (A *saeculum* was a period of hundred years. By a bogus calculation endorsed by the custodians of the Sibylline books, this was lengthened to a hundred and ten years in order to coincide with the tenth anniversary of the Principate in 17 BC.) Horace's hymn, which was performed by a chorus of boys and girls, formed the climax to a three-day celebration. 'Now the Mede fears an enemy that is mighty by land and by sea, now he fears the Alban axes', he wrote. 'Now Faith and Peace and Honour and Respect and neglected Virtue dare to return, and blessed Abundance with her cornucopia is in evidence.' We know that the hymn met with Augustus' full satisfaction because he ordered it to be inscribed. It was probably the high point of Horace's career.

Using the good offices of wealthy patrons of poetry such as Maecenas and Messalla, Augustus also sought, more presumptuously, to commission a grandiose epic that would celebrate the establishment of the Principate. Horace and Propertius both declined, but Vergil agreed, apparently on condition that Augustus should not be the central figure of his narrative. He may have put forward the argument that the battle of Actium was hardly a fit subject for epic treatment, since halfway through it Cleopatra and Mark Antony ignominiously turned tail and fled. Instead Vergil chose to focus on the dutiful self-sacrifice of Aeneas, the founding father of the Roman people, which he presented as a typological link to Augustus. Though he bestows incidental praise on Augustus by way of the comments that he ascribes to Jupiter and others, it is questionable whether he intended his poem to be interpreted as an unqualified endorsement of the Principate.

It goes without saying that the services of Horace and Vergil were hardly critical to the success of the Principate, though the fact that men of such talent could be co-opted into making mildly supportive references to his rule may have helped defuse any tendency towards subversion on the part of the intellectual élite.

Thousands mob chief!

The élite apart, there can be no doubt that the average Roman would have been profoundly grateful to Augustus for the restoration of stability and prosperity, following as it did upon the heels of a period of intense and prolonged civil war. When he returned to Italy in 19 BC, after a three-year tour of the eastern provinces, a huge crowd turned out to greet him at Brundisium (modern Brindisi) in southern Italy. As Augustus journeyed north, the Senate travelled south to Campania, where it gave him its formal welcome. In response to the tumultuous outpouring of relief and rejoicing from the adulatory crowd, the Senate dedicated an altar to Fortuna Redux ('Fortune, the Returning Leader' or 'Fortune the Bringer Home') near the Porta Capena through which the Appian Way issued. A conventional attention-seeker would have milked this moment for all it was worth. Characteristically Augustus sought to downplay it. He declined a triumph, accepting only its insignia instead, and entered the capital by night so as to avoid creating a public disturbance.[5] The day of his return, celebrated as the Augustalia, was incorporated into the festival calendar.

When Augustus stood for election as Supreme Pontiff in 12 BC, more people travelled to Rome from all over Italy than had done so at any time previously, as he proudly recorded in the public record of his achievements known as the *Res Gestae* (see pp. 61-2 below). It's likely that spontaneous gestures of support attended him throughout his reign. Suetonius tells us that when a group of Alexandrians who were on board ship learnt that he was in their region, they put on white robes and burnt incense in his honour. They did so, they explained, because they owed to Augustus 'their entire liberty and prosperity'.[6]

Simply divine!

It was inevitable that moves should be made to deify Augustus during his lifetime as a way of marking his unique status. Vergil declared him to be a 'divinely sent saviour',[7] while Horace claimed that he was destined for heaven.[8] Augustus responded by allowing himself to be worshipped as a god only by non-Romans inhabiting parts of the Greek-speaking East where there already existed a tradition of ruler worship – and then only in conjunction with the goddess Roma, the personification of Rome's power. Herod the Great, for instance, was permitted to dedicate three temples to Roma and Augustus in Judaea – at Caesarea Maritima, Sebaste and Panias.

In the capital itself, however, Augustus carefully avoided any suggestion that he might be tacitly conniving at his own deification. For instance, he refused to allow his statue to be carried in public processions as was customary in the case of gods, and he declined to sit on a golden throne. He also prohibited Agrippa from consecrating the Pantheon, the centrepiece to his building programme in the Campus Martius, to himself. (Instead Agrippa dedicated it to Augustus' divine ancestors, Mars, Venus and the deified Julius.) He even ostentatiously ordered the melting down of silver statues that had been set up in the capital in his honour and used the proceeds to manufacture gold tripods which he then dedicated to Palatine Apollo.[9]

Following the posthumous deification of his adoptive father, Augustus did, however, assume the title '*divi filius*' or 'son of the deified'. An annual sacrifice was performed before the Ara Pacis (Altar of Peace) in the Campus Martius, at which he was commended as the father of the 'Roman peace' or *pax Romana*. From 30 BC onwards libations were offered at private and public banquets to his *genius*, the power which resided in the head of a Roman household, in his official capacity as head of state. Being entirely informal, it avoided causing the offence to which it would have given rise, had it been placed in the hands of an official priesthood.

Chief confesses: Principate was a one-man show!

Few posthumous publications in the history of celebrity have made such a blatant bid for attention as the inscription known today as the *Res Gestae* (Achievements). The inscription was probably promulgated around the time of Augustus' death throughout the entire Empire, though all extant copies happen to come from the eastern province of Galatia. Both in tone and character, the *Res Gestae* reflects the unstated but underlying ethos of the Principate, by attributing every social, economic and military success to the First Citizen, in much the same way that Augustus did in his lifetime. Its self-serving tone is further emphasized by the use of the first person singular, which is very unusual in inscriptions.[10]

Augustus mentions his foremost military strategist, Agrippa, merely in his capacity as fellow colleague in the priestly college of the *quindecimviri*, the fifteen custodians of the Sibylline books. The only other generals whom he refers to by name are his grandsons Gaius and Lucius, and his stepson, the future Emperor Tiberius. Several victories are ascribed to anonymous legates acting under Augustus' 'order and auspices'. Caesar's assassins are alluded to obliquely and contemptuously as 'the men who butchered my father'. There is no direct mention of his hated adversaries, Mark Antony and Cleopatra. Notable, too, is the absence of any reference to his wife Livia, who in a different cultural climate might have expected a brief tribute to her 'unflagging devotion and support' (*vel sim.*) during their fifty-three years of (not entirely) blissful married life. He does, however, scrupulously list all the offices and titles which he declined, above all the dictatorship. His modesty, he immoderately proclaims, knew no bounds.

The message underlying the *Res Gestae* rings out with deafening clarity. 'It was I, Augustus, who rescued Rome from civil war, it was I who restored the Republic, it was I who saved the people from the disasters of famine, fire and flood, it was I who immeasurably improved Rome's amenities, it was I who doubled the size of her Empire, and it was I who established peace throughout its boundaries. And what's more, there's never been anyone like me.' The document begins: 'At the age of nineteen, taking advice from no one and at my own expense, I raised an army with which I restored the liberty of the Republic when it was repressed by tyranny' – Augustus' presumptuous claim that he single-handedly overcame Caesar's assassins. Towards the end it states: 'In my sixth and seventh consulships, after I had extinguished civil conflict, at the time when, by universal consent, I had complete power, I transferred the Republic from my control into the jurisdiction of the Senate and the Roman People' – his no less presumptuous claim that he had restored the Republic to its previous condition of health.

Though scholars differ as to the identity of his main target group, it's not unlikely that he was chiefly addressing Romans born after the establishment of the Principate. After all, it was they who were most susceptible to the image of Augustus as an exemplary public servant, for the obvious reason that they were too young to know any better.

Crowds swoon at feet of emperor's nephew!

Augustus' superstar status encouraged his subjects to concentrate all their hopes, fears, aspirations and anxieties upon the person of one man. Future emperors would respond to their role as the nation's saviour according to their differing personalities. His immediate successor, the publicity-shy Tiberius, forbade all manifestations of excessive devotion. In particular he rejected the Senate's proposal to change the name of September to Tiberius and of October to Livius (in honour of his mother Livia).[11]

Even so, nothing demonstrates more emphatically that the emperor could now alone claim superstar status than the fact that Tiberius took pains not to allow the attention of his subjects drift elsewhere. He was especially wary of his charismatic nephew and adopted son, Germanicus Caesar. In AD 19 Germanicus found it prudent to issue a formal rebuke to the Alexandrians after they had given him a tumultuous welcome for alleviating a severe food shortage. He also threatened to reduce the number of his public appearances, if they continued to hail him as their saviour.[12] Germanicus sought to limit the scope of his celebrity, we should note, not because he was afflicted with a thoroughly un-Roman sense of innate modesty, but because he judged it to be in his best interests not to aggravate the suspicions of his paranoid uncle, who viewed his popularity with deep suspicion.

Unlike the reclusive Tiberius, the Emperor Nero did everything he could to hog the limelight, instituting games in his own name, re-naming April *Neroneus*, and building the greatest imperial palace of all time, the *Domus Aurea* (Golden House), on the Palatine Hill. At the time of his death he was even on the point of re-naming Rome 'Neropolis' (see further p. 75 below).

Former imperial secretary tells all!

With the rise to public prominence of the imperial family came the tittle-tattle so beloved of the imperial biographer Suetonius, one-time secretary to the Emperor Hadrian. Of the twelve Caesars whose lives he records, only Vitellius and Titus escape censure. The rest, variously charged with lasciviousness, extravagance, cruelty, slothfulness and greed, present a gallery of dysfunctional misfits and demonic sociopaths. Of Julius Caesar, Suetonius reports a quip by the Elder Curio to the effect that he was 'Every woman's man, and every man's woman', and notes that he had a passion for his colleagues' wives. Of Augustus, that the price of his adoption by Julius Caesar was to submit to buggery by his great-uncle. Of Tiberius, that he was a pederast who trained little boys to suck his penis under water. Of Caligula, that he committed incest with each of his three sisters in turn. Of Claudius, that he never rose from his couch except drunken and gorged. Of Nero, that he was fond of gnawing at the private parts of prisoners bound at the stake, committed incest with his mother, and kicked his pregnant wife Poppaea to death. Of Galba, that he enjoyed being buggered by hefty men. Of Otho, that he was a transvestite and transsexual. Of Domitian, that he consorted with the most disgusting prostitutes he could lay his hands on. How much of all this is true? We will of course never know. No doubt it was laced with the kind of fantasy that any ordinary Roman might have dreamt up – and even have dreamt himself doing – were he lucky enough to find himself in the emperor's sandals.

Suetonius wisely elected to bring his biographies to a halt with Domitian, who died twenty years before his own patron Hadrian succeeded to the throne. Had he continued with his researches, we can be confident that he would have found no shortage of salacious gossip to relate about Domitian's successors. Plenty more factoids and tittle-tattle about the later emperors and claimants to the imperial throne are found in the thirty biographies that go under the title of the *Historia Augusta*, covering the period from Hadrian to Numerianus (AD 117-284), which were probably written around the middle of the fourth century.

The only instrument that the Senate had at its disposal for controlling imperial excess was the posthumous passing of a decree known as *damnatio memoriae*. This commonly included the destruction of the emperor's image, the erasing of his name from inscriptions, and the abolition of his decrees. Its victims included Domitian, Commodus and Elagabalus. The message that the Senate sought to send to would-be imperial malefactors was clear: fame and infamy are mutually exclusive. The paradoxical and unintended consequence was that the memory of their infamy lived on.

Afterlife

Augustus began to tend his posthumous reputation from the mid-thirties BC onwards, most obviously by publishing his speeches, no doubt after carefully editing them. He also revised the *Res Gestae* several times during the course of his life. Though he came in for some criticism in the century after his death, notably from the historian Tacitus, he was generally praised for his character and accomplishments – 'a most circumspect and wise ruler' in Suetonius' considered judgement.[13] His immortality was guaranteed by the re-naming of *Sextilis*, originally the sixth month of the year, as *Augustus*, and by the longevity of the Principate itself. 'Augustus' became the chief imperial title and was assumed by all later emperors with the exception of Tiberius, who used it only in official documents. Similarly 'Augusta' was occasionally bestowed on the emperor's wife and on other members of the imperial family. The first to be honoured in this way was Livia, who assumed this title on the death of Augustus. The second was the Younger Agrippina, who assumed the title during the lifetime of her husband, the Emperor Claudius.

'Augustus' was bestowed upon a number of military units and cities, and it survives to this day vestigially in several European place names. They include Augusta Praetoria (modern Aosta in the Italian Alps), Augusta Raurica (modern Augst near Basle), Augusta Traiana (modern Stara Zagora in Bulgaria), Augusta Vindelicorum (modern Augsberg), and Augustodunum (modern Autun).

The Sports Star

It's just a job. Grass grows, birds fly, waves pound the sand. I beat people up.

Muhammad Ali, boxer

Athletics was the only activity that enabled a talented Greek of no social distinction to achieve something approaching celebrity status in the Archaic and Classical periods. As the Phaeacian prince Laodamas says to Odysseus as he invites him to participate in their local games, 'You seem to be an athlete. No one achieves greater renown (*kleos*) throughout his lifetime than the man who wins victory with his feet or his hands.'[1] The world of Odysseus in fact mirrored Homer's own, in that the reputation of top athletes spread far and wide. The first name to enter the historical record is that of a humble baker named Coroebus of Elis, who won the footrace at the first celebration of the Olympic Games in 776 BC. Coroebus' achievement has come down to us because it was the practice to identify each Olympiad by the name of the victor in the stade (*c.* 200 metres) footrace. There could scarcely be a more effective way to publicize the achievement of someone who had previously been a complete nonentity.

Equestrian events were the preserve of wealthy aristocrats, since they alone could afford to finance racing stables. The hoi polloi could compete only in footraces and body-contact sports, namely boxing, wrestling and *pankration*, a combination of boxing, wrestling and judo. The most prestigious games were the Olympic, Pythian, Nemean and Isthmian, which were known collectively as the 'stephanitic' or crown games since the prize for victory in each case was a simple crown of leaves – olive at Olympia, laurel at Delphi, celery at Nemea and pine at Isthmia – though other prestigious rewards awaited victors on their return home. Becoming an Olympic victor or *Olympionikês* was the highest honour, and the biggest stars were the *periodonikai* or circuit victors – contestants, that is, who achieved victories at all four venues in a row, a feat that has been aptly compared to winning four Grand Slam tournaments in tennis in the same season. Women competed in a shortened footrace at Olympia in games held in honour of Hera, but there is no clear evidence for their participation at any other major festival before the Imperial era.

Though the sports stars of the sixth and fifth centuries BC seem to have enjoyed greater celebrity than those of the period that followed, such was the continuing prestige of the games in the Hellenistic era that even the Ptolemies who ruled Egypt deigned to compete in athletic and equestrian events. In the first to third centuries AD interest in the games revived, largely as a result of imperial patronage. Although the Romans refrained from participating in athletics, they did compete in both equestrian and musical events, and none with more eagerness than the Emperor Nero. The most popular sport in imperial times, and, equally, the one that produced the biggest celebrities and the most devoted fans, was chariot-racing.

Victor's daughter weds celebrity physician!

Apart from the poems of Pindar, Simonides and Bacchylides, most of our evidence about Greek athletes dates from Roman times. Interest is focused on a handful of sports stars, whose superhuman feats of prowess were still mesmerizing the imagination half a millennium after their deaths. Though many of the anecdotes that built around their reputations were apocryphal, we need hardly doubt that they had in their day been larger-than-life personalities. Probably, too, some of them evinced a talent for showmanship that more than matched their physical prowess.

Arguably the most famous Greek athlete of all time was a wrestler named Milo, who came from Croton in south Italy, a city famous for the number of star athletes that it produced. Milo's career began in 536 BC when he was victorious in the boys' category at Olympia. He went on to win at least six Olympic crowns in a row and was six times circuit victor. In all he won seven crowns in the Pythian Games, ten in the Isthmian, and nine in the Nemean. Milo's reputation even spread beyond the borders of the Greek world. Herodotus reports that a fellow-citizen from Croton named Democedes paid a considerable sum of money for the privilege of becoming engaged to his daughter.

Democedes, who was a famous physician and an accomplished attention-seeker in his own right, sought the connection with the wrestler
to prove to the Persian king Darius, from whose clutches he had
recently escaped, that he was esteemed as much in Greece as in
Persia, knowing as he did that 'the king held the name of Milo in high
honour'.[2] In other words, Democedes calculated that becoming engaged to the daughter of the world's most famous athlete was a good
way to impress the world's most famous king.

Another highly celebrated athlete was Theagenes of Thasos, who at
the age of eight is said to have removed a bronze statue from its plinth
in the agora of his home town and to have carried it home on his
shoulders. The Thasians were on the point of lynching him when a
respected elder stepped forward and instructed the boy to return the
statue to its proper place. He complied and 'at once became famed for
his strength, as his accomplishment was the talk of all Greece', the
travel-writer Pausanias tells us.[3] Theagenes was equally skilled in
both boxing and *pankration*. He later became successful as a runner
as well, eager to rival Achilles' reputation for swiftness of foot. Though
he became an Olympic victor only twice, he is said to have collected
one thousand three hundred crowns overall, most of them at the local
games that were celebrated in this period throughout the Greek-
speaking world.

An anecdote about an all-in wrestler called Dorieus, who fought
alongside the Spartans during the Peloponnesian War, is indicative of
the enormous prestige that sports stars enjoyed in the late fifth
century BC. Dorieus, who had been taken prisoner by the Athenians in
a sea battle, was about to be executed when his captors discovered his
true identity. In deference to his renown, they released him unharmed
– an early instance of the preferential treatment that is routinely
handed out to celebrities in the contemporary world.

Brutal tyrant 'wonderful father' claims poet!

From just before the middle of the sixth century BC to just after the
middle of the fifth, aristocratic victors in equestrian contests were in
the habit of commissioning a victory ode or *epinikion* in their own
honour from a poet who specialized in the writing of such verse. A
victory ode was a choral poem, typically about a hundred lines in

length, which was set to music and sung to the accompaniment of dancing. Some *epinikia* received their first performance at the victory celebration following the games. Others, particularly the more elaborate ones, were first performed at the victor's homecoming celebration (see below). Repeat performances probably took place throughout the victor's lifetime to keep the memory of his achievement before the public gaze. Copies of the ode were retained by his family and also, in some cases, by his native city. One such ode, which was composed on behalf of a boxer named Diagoras of Rhodes, who won the Olympic crown in 464 BC, was even inscribed in letters of gold and preserved inside the temple of Athena at Lindus on Rhodes.[4]

Relatively low-key though this medium of self-promotion might seem to us, its importance in the history of celebrity can hardly be exaggerated. Typically an *epinikion* suggested that the victor had acquired a quasi-heroic status – one that put him on a par with the most distinguished of his ancestors. The most celebrated exponent of this art-form was the Boeotian poet Pindar, whose long career spanned the entire first half of the fifth century BC. Pindar's clients were primarily powerful tyrants and distinguished aristocrats. The majority were the owners of horses who had been victorious in equestrian events. They included the tyrants Hieron of Syracuse and Theron of Acragas, Hieron's general Chromios, Theron's brother Xenocrates, and Arkesilas, king of Cyrene. They all expected Pindar to present them in a highly flattering light. He never disappointed. Rather, he went out of his way to massage their shady reputations. He lauded the violent and unscrupulous Hieron, for instance, for being 'gentle to his people, unenvious towards the nobles, and a wonderful father to foreign guests'.[5]

The popularity of the *epinikion* sheds an instructive light on the keen competitiveness that underlay relations between men of wealth and power throughout the Greek-speaking world. It is interesting, too, that Pindar, who came from an aristocratic background, saw himself not as their lowly hireling, but almost on an equal footing, as we see from the fact that he often compares himself to the victor whose success he is celebrating.

The genre also provides us with insight into the Greek awareness of the psychological dangers of celebrity, since the poems regularly include warnings to the victors not to let their fame go to their heads.

This advice, appropriate in any age, had particular urgency for the Greeks, owing to their belief that excessive human prosperity invited the envy of the gods. It also testifies to the extremely high profile that a victor at the panhellenic games attained. Not all epinician poets sought to protect their patrons from the excesses of their own celebrity, however. Pindar's slightly older contemporary Simonides, who was commissioned to celebrate the accomplishments of a boxer named Glaucus of Carystus, incautiously boasted that his patron surpassed both Pollux and Heracles in his exceptional physical prowess.

Following the death of Pindar in *c.* 446 BC, the fashion for commissioning *epinikia* died out. It certainly wasn't the case that wealthy aristocrats had become less competitive, so the demise of the genre probably reflects a change in artistic taste. Henceforth the preferred method of self-advertisement was the victory statue, which already had a long-established tradition. Such statues were erected in the victor's home town and, with considerably more visibility, in the panhellenic sanctuary where the victory took place. The first Olympic victor to be so honoured was a boxer named Praxidamas of Aegina in 544 BC. Tradition relates that only three-times Olympic victors were permitted to reproduce their own likenesses, and further that the statue could not be bigger than life-size. Top-notch artists competed for the commissions at Olympia, eager to showcase their art in Greece's most prestigious and most frequented public space. The practice continued well into the Imperial era. A pancratiast named Marcus Aurelius Asclepiades, whose career lasted from AD 181 to 196, boasted on his statue base, 'I was the unvanquished, the unshakeable, the unchallenged winner on the athletic circuit, winning all the contests that I entered.'[6] Asclepiades made enough money to retire at the age of twenty-five – an indication of just how much wealth top sporting personalities could earn in later antiquity.

Cash bonuses for Olympic victors!

According to legend, it was the Athenian lawgiver Solon who took the pioneering step of forging the link between sporting fame and fortune by awarding cash bonuses to victors in the Olympic and Isthmian Games – five hundred drachmas to the former and a hundred to the latter. Five hundred drachmas, though hardly a king's ransom, were certainly enough to enable the recipient to become a professional. Other cities followed suit. This not only enhanced the celebrity of the most accomplished athletes by according them privileged status, but also enabled talented men of humble origins to choose athletics as a career.

Cash bonuses were not the only form of recognition that victors in the crown games received. On the contrary, Greek states aggressively touted their achievements throughout their lifetime, as Pindar indicates in his observation that 'The victor has fair weather for the rest of his life on account of the contests.'[7] This began with a grandiose civic reception. A twice-crowned Olympic victor in the stade race named Exainetus of Acragas (modern Agrigento) in Sicily, for instance, was escorted into the city by three hundred chariots drawn by white horses. Other privileges included free meals at public expense, exemption from taxes, the entitlement to a state pension, and the right to sit in the front row at the theatre and at state-sponsored games. Spartan victors had the distinction of standing beside the kings in battle. On a Thespian war memorial victors in the Olympic and Pythian Games are identified as a separate category among the dead.[8] Though a few spoilsports like Socrates derided the practice of rewarding sports stars, most Greeks, like most people today, were content to bask in the reflected glory of their compatriots.

Ardent fan's self-immolation!

Because of its essentially aristocratic character, chariot-racing had a rather limited following in the Greek world, even though victory in this event bestowed considerable prestige in aristocratic circles. The drivers who risked life and limb are rarely mentioned in the *epinikia*, however, and rarely if at all did they become celebrities. Instead it was the owners of the chariot teams who received the credit and the kudos. Chariot-racing was therefore the one major sporting event that women could enter, and as such it provided an acceptable avenue for their self-promotion. The first woman to win the chariot-race at Olympia was Cynisca of Sparta, who proudly commemorated her victory in 396 BC with these stirring words:

The kings of Sparta are my fathers and brothers. I, Cynisca, winning with my chariot and swift horses, have set up this

72

statue. I declare that I am the only woman in all Greece to take this crown.[9]

Though Greek-style chariot-races were still being held on the Greek mainland as late as the second century AD, by then the sport had long since ceased to attract much attention. Roman-style chariot-racing, the origins of which extended back to the regal period, had become the most popular sport, and indeed the most popular form of entertainment throughout the Roman Empire. Charioteers were even referred to as *histriones* or 'stage actors'. Spectators would queue all night for a seat in the Circus Maximus, located in a flat plain in Rome between the Aventine and Palatine hills, which was thought to have had a capacity of two hundred and fifty thousand. Major metropoleis, including Alexandria, Antioch, Berytus, Caesarea Maritima, Carthage, Constantinople, Laodicea and Tyre, all had circuses which could accommodate at least a hundred thousand. In total, there were about a hundred and seventy-five circuses scattered throughout the Empire, many with seating capacities of twenty thousand or more.

Hardly any celebrities in antiquity generated such fanatical devotion as charioteers. When one named Felix was cremated in 70 AD, a fan of his was so distraught that he threw himself onto Felix's funeral pyre and was burnt alive. (Interestingly Pliny the Elder, who is our source for this story, claims to have read about it in a daily gazette known as the *acta diurna*.)[10] Another charioteer named Flavius Scorpus, who died at the age of twenty-seven in AD 98, is the subject of no fewer than seven of Martial's epigrams.

The popularity of chariot-racing was due largely to the fact that the spotlight rested unwaveringly upon the charioteers, many of whom were no doubt professional dare-devils. Their celebrity was so great that members of the Roman élite participated in the sport, the most conspicuous example being the Emperor Nero. What strengthened the partisan spirit of their fans was the fact that in Rome and Constantinople chariot-racing was in effect a team event, since the charioteers were identified by their racing colours – the Greens, the Blues, the Whites and the Reds. And as with soccer fans today, passions among the supporters of the rival colours ran so high that outbreaks of violence were not uncommon.

The career of a certain Caius Apuleius Diocles, who was born in

Lusitania (approximately modern Portugal), is exemplary. Diocles' accomplishments are preserved in a lengthy inscription engraved by his fans and stable companions in AD 146. In it he is described as 'the champion of all charioteers … (who) excelled the charioteers of all the stables who ever participated in the races of the circus games'. Diocles began driving for the Whites, transferred to the Greens six years later, and finally joined up with the Reds three years after that. Though it's unclear what induced him to switch allegiance, financial considerations were probably to the fore. In the course of a career that lasted nearly a quarter of a century Diocles competed in 4,257 races, winning 1,462 times. In prize money he amassed the fabulous sum of 35,863,120 sesterces, which surely made him one of the highest earners of his day. The fact that detailed records of the races were preserved (we are told, for instance, that Diocles 'took the lead and won 815 times, came from behind and won 67 times, won under handicap 36 times', etc.) must have greatly bolstered the celebrity of the most skilful drivers, whose names would therefore have been familiar to aficionados throughout the Empire.[11] Another famous charioteer called Publius Aelius Gutta Calpurnianus won in a single race almost half of the annual salary of a highly paid tutor to Augustus' grandsons.[12] (Some things in life never change.) Like other celebrities, star charioteers enjoyed the confidence of the imperial court. The Emperor Elagabalus (reigned AD 217-22), who was admittedly somewhat deranged, appointed a charioteer named Gordius to a top governmental post.[13]

The fanaticism aroused by chariot-racing in the eastern part of the Roman Empire is attested by the great hippodrome in Constantinople, which was rebuilt by the Emperor Constantine in the first half of the fourth century AD with an estimated seating capacity of 100,000. Its importance in the West is revealed in a letter written by the Ostrogothic Emperor Theodoric (reigned 493-526) to Faustus, his prefect in Rome, in which he justifies his decision to award a prestigious government grant to a charioteer named Thomas:

When the charioteer Thomas came recently from the East, after due consideration We bestowed on him a reasonable allowance, until We could prove his skill and character. Since he is acknowledged to have achieved the highest position in this sport and since of his own free will he has left his country and chosen the seat of Our Empire as his sphere of activity, We have adjudged him worthy of a monthly grant, so that We might leave no doubt of Our opinion of a man who has recognized the primacy of Italy in the world.[14]

In expressing such deep gratitude to Thomas for gracing the capital with his presence, the emperor is all but putting him on an equal footing with himself. As the letter indicates, he regards him as a man of upstanding character, capable of serving as a valuable role model to his numerous fans, who were, as we have seen, endemically prone to factiousness and rioting. Whether Theodoric succeeded in enticing Thomas to his capital at Ravenna for a well-publicized handshake on the steps of the imperial palace is, sadly, not recorded.

Superstar seeks celebrity status!

Being an imperial superstar was not the same as being a celebrity, as we see from the career of the Emperor Nero, who has been described as 'the Elvis of ancient Rome'. Nero had a pathological craving for recognition both as a sports star and as an entertainer. In Suetonius' words, his predominant characteristics included 'a thirst for popular support (*popularitas*) and a jealousy of all who caught the public eye by any means whatsoever'.[15] Whatever the exact meaning of *popularitas* in this context, it was clearly something quite different from the *auctoritas* of an Augustus. Such was Nero's eagerness to acquire celebrity status that his portrait head on coins for the year AD 64 may actually have even been influenced by the hairstyle of actors or charioteers.

Nero made his stage début as a lyre player at Neapolis (modern Naples) in AD 64. He evidently chose Neapolis, a Greek foundation, in the expectation that its largely foreign population would appreciate his musical talents for their own sake. His performances were attended by a claque of 'young men of the equestrian order and more than five thousand sturdy youths from among the plebs', who applauded in unison wherever he sang.[16] Though claques were a well-known feature of the Roman theatre, the number and sturdiness of Nero's fans would have done much to intimidate those among his audience who might otherwise have been tempted to cheer ill-advisedly for any of the other competitors. In addition, a corps of knights known as the Augustiani 'kept up a din of applause day and night, bestowing divine epithets on his voice and beauty'.[17] If the applause that greeted Nero's performances in the theatre turned out to be somewhat ragged or lacklustre, as, for instance, in the remoter parts of Italy, soldiers posted in the auditorium would beat the spectators 'so that no time would be wasted in irregular shouting or sluggish silence'.[18]

Nero also appeared on stage as a tragic actor in a variety of melodramatic roles including 'Canace in labour, Orestes the matricide, Oedipus blinded, and Hercules mad'.[19] We need hardly doubt that he would have milked the emotions of his audience for all they were worth. Today we would probably classify him as a first-class ham.

The upper classes deeply resented Nero's exhibitionism, which they judged to be unbecoming to the dignity of an emperor. Their resentment may have inspired the famous anecdote that Nero played the lyre while Rome was burning. But though Suetonius and Tacitus both heap scorn on Nero for craving the cheap celebrity of a showbiz personality, neither of them disguises the fact that he took his stage appearances very seriously, even if there was hardly any doubt about the outcome of the contests. In particular they admit that he suffered from stage fright and they acknowledge that he awaited the judges' verdict with trepidation.[20] Evidently Nero craved to be appreciated for qualities that had nothing to do with his imperial title and rank.

Nero's greatest ambition was to be a victor in the four-horse chariot-race, which he regarded as a sport worthy of kings. In 66 AD he went to Greece, after ordering that the four crown games be held in the same year so that he would not have to interrupt his busy schedule. (The fact that he was thrown from his chariot at Olympia and forced to retire before the end of the race did not prevent the judges from awarding him the victory.) Having added to the clamour that greeted his victory at the Isthmian Games by announcing the liberation of Greece, he returned home in the guise of a general celebrating a triumph.

A few months later Nero was assassinated. His name was expunged from the Olympic records and his sculptural portraits were destroyed – just deserts, it might be said, for one of the most outrageous attention-seekers in history. We need to bear in mind, however, that there was more to Nero's craving for public attention than meets the eye, for it enabled him to present himself to his subjects as a popular idol. The goodwill of the plebs was in fact vital to him, as he received little support either from the army or from the senatorial and equestrian orders. Though his ploy ultimately failed, his efforts argue the continuing importance of celebrity as a political weapon in the Roman world.[21]

Afterlife

The quintessential athlete in folk memory was the wrestler Milo, whose name became synonymous initially with heroic self-sacrifice and later with asinine brawn. The historian Diodorus reports that it was due primarily to his superhuman strength that his fellow-citizens secured a victory over the neighbouring city of Sybaris, despite being outnumbered three to one. The geographer Strabo claims that Milo saved the lives of some Pythagorean philosophers when a pillar in the building in which they were sitting collapsed. From the second century AD onwards, however, his reputation suffered in line with the contempt that came to be levelled against athletes by medical writers such as Galen. The excessive rigour and artificiality of their training programmes were roundly condemned as both injurious to health and a pointless waste of energy. They thus fell early victims to an all too familiar psychological disorder known today as *machismo nervosa*, which induces an excessive commitment to the goal of transforming one's physical image. Milo now became a figure of fun, remembered more for his abnormal appetite than for his stirring acts of prowess. Legend recorded that he carried a four-year-old bull on his shoulders around the stadium at Olympia, before devouring its whole carcass at one sitting.[22]

The boxer Diagoras of Rhodes became symbolic of the fleeting nature of human fortune. 'Die, Diagoras, for you will not ascend to heaven,' a Spartan is said to have remarked when two of Diagoras' sons were crowned Olympian victors on the same day, the implication being that Diagoras had reached the summit of felicity that was permitted to mortals in this life.[23]

Probably the athlete whose reputation burned most brightly in later times was the pancratiast Theagenes of Thasos, although tales were told of his gargantuan appetite as well. Alexander the Great saw fit to erect a statue of himself beside that of the boxer at Olympia. Pausanias reports that he was worshipped as a healing hero 'not only among the Greeks but also among the barbarians'.[24] As the majority of healing heroes received cult in only one location, Theagenes must have been credited with extraordinary powers. A circular monument dated *c*. AD 100, found in the agora at Thasos, verifies Pausanias' report.

Several other Greek athletes were awarded heroic honours after their death, testifying to their enduring fame. The most bizarre example involves Cleomedes of Astypalaea, a boxer who was stripped of his Olympic crown in 492 BC, probably on the grounds of cheating. On his return home, Cleomedes massacred sixty children by pulling down one of the pillars supporting their school building. While fleeing from his irate fellow-countrymen, he made his escape by jumping inside a box and in so doing mysteriously disappeared. The Astypalaeans inquired of Delphi what had happened to him and were told, 'Cleomedes was the last of the heroes. Honour him with sacrifices, as he is no longer mortal.'[25] The anecdote perhaps served as a warning of the destructive psychological consequences that may befall a celebrity who experiences a very public shaming.

Though the death of Nero was for the most part greeted with public rejoicing, a few genuinely mourned his passing, as we learn from the fact that flowers continued to be placed on his grave twice a year long after his death and that statues of him were erected on the Rostra (or speakers' platform) in the Roman Forum. The Emperor Otho permitted busts of Nero to be re-erected and Otho's successor Vitellius made funerary offerings at Nero's grave. At least two men claiming to be Nero made appearances in the East after his death. A possible third turned up almost twenty years later.[26] These Nero look-alikes evidently hoped not only to cash in on the emperor's celebrity but also to appropriate the mantle of his power. In the literary tradition Nero quickly became the personification of monstrosity. Even so, there was a degree of ambivalence. In a treatise entitled 'Concerning the slowness of divine punishment' Plutarch pictures demons forcing the souls of the evil dead into new bodies. Just as the demons are about to fashion Nero into a viper, a voice commands them to transfer his soul into a 'singing animal that inhabits swamps and marshes' instead, in recognition of the fact that he had granted the Greeks their freedom.[27]

The Celebrity Guru

> Ten thousand fools proclaim themselves into obscurity, while one wise man forgets himself into immortality.
>
> Dr Martin Luther King, Jr, civil rights campaigner

Already in the *Odyssey* we hear of skilled professionals whose expertise was valued beyond the confines of their local community and who were 'summoned from afar' by those who sought their services.[1] These itinerants, namely seers, physicians, carpenters and bards, were the first celebrities, albeit minor ones, whose reputations owed nothing to birth or privilege. This was certainly true of the poet Hesiod, for instance, who claims to have received his vocation while tending his flocks in the foothills of Mount Helicon, and there is no reason to suppose that his social status among bards as a whole was in any way unique.

Homer does not give us any hint as to the distance that a renowned seer, physician, carpenter or bard might travel in the course of his career. In historical times, however, itinerant professionals travelled vast distances and were treated as visiting dignitaries, very much like their modern counterparts. Though they remained largely reliant on the patronage of men of wealth and influence, some were judged to offer such valuable services to the public that city-states vied with one another to hire their services. In the Imperial period the ultimate accolade was the patronage of the emperor himself, with Rome acting as a powerful magnet for talented and ambitious individuals eager to make a name for themselves. The attention which the celebrity guru received was perhaps not unlike that accorded to leading twentieth-century intellectuals, including Bertrand Russell, A.J.P. Taylor and Aldous Huxley.[2]

Big name sophist in town!

Around the middle of the fifth century BC a handful of highly gifted self-promoters made an appearance on the Greek intellectual scene as itinerant teachers. Known as sophists (a name derived from the Greek word *sophos* meaning 'sage' or 'expert'), they acquired panhellenic reputations. Their phenomenal success is one of the most extraordinary events in the history of celebrity. Though the sophists earned their livelihood principally by teaching their pupils the art of rhetoric, they also drew large crowds by lecturing on the burning philosophical issues of the day.

Their impact on Greek culture is all the more remarkable in view of the fact that the movement to which they belonged lasted barely a generation. Although we know the names of some twenty-six sophists, only five made it into the big league: Protagoras, who came from Abdera on the borders of Thrace; Gorgias, from Leontini in Sicily; Prodicus, who was born on the island of Ceos; Hippias from Elis in the Peloponnese; and Thrasymachus from Chalcedon in what is today Turkey. Though none was an Athenian, all gravitated towards Athens, which, with its Assembly and law courts, provided the best opportunity for showcasing the results of their rhetorical training, as well as being a centre of intellectual activity.

As we see from Plato's *Protagoras*, the arrival of a celebrity sophist caused a considerable buzz among the cognoscenti. At the beginning of the dialogue a youth named Hippocrates is so keen to meet his idol that he arrives breathless at Socrates' house long before dawn to inform him that the great man is in town. True to character, the young Socrates is underwhelmed by the news and only with some reluctance agrees to sally forth to meet him. As was common practice among sophists, Protagoras was residing at the house of a wealthy aristocrat. He had arrived in Athens with a retinue of admirers, who no doubt enhanced the aura of his personality. Plato wryly observes that they 'had been brought from the numerous cities which he visits, enchanted by a voice which is equal to that of Orpheus'.[3] Hippias and Prodicus also happened to be sojourning in Athens when Protagoras arrived, so it may well be that sophists co-ordinated their itineraries to create a particularly big splash. Their most generous patron was a wealthy aristocrat called Callias, whose house provides the setting for the dialogue in question. Callias is said to have spent more money sponsoring sophists than all other Athenians put together. No doubt his reputation benefited from its association with intellectuals of international repute. Sponsoring sophists, in other words, was yet another way in which an ambitious aristocrat competed with his peers for attention. The sophists did not confine their teaching to the major cities. Hippias, for instance, claimed to have earned twenty minas by lecturing to the inhabitants of a small Sicilian village.[4]

Though most of their instruction took place in small classes and seminars, the sophists also gave display-lectures known as *epideixeis*. The best-attended of these were delivered in theatres and other public venues, which suggests that they attracted crowds numbering in the thousands, possibly even in the tens of thousands. Perhaps to emphasize their historic tie with the rhapsodes (see p. 106 below), they would dress in purple robes when they delivered lectures. Hippias is known to have given *epideixeis* at Olympia while the games were being held, which suggests that he may have been competing for a prize in rhetorical display. Gorgias, too, spoke at both the Olympic and the Pythian Games.

The sophists were in the business of making serious money. Gorgias became so wealthy that he set up a gold statue of himself in the temple of Pythian Apollo in Delphi – the first gold statue of a human being to be erected in Greece – while Protagoras is said to have earned more money than Pheidias and ten other sculptors combined.

Wacko philosopher in screwball comedy!

Tradition has it that at the first performance of Aristophanes' comic masterpiece *Clouds* (423 BC), which gives star billing to the philosopher Socrates, some foreigners in the audience began whispering among themselves, 'Who is this Socrates?' Whereupon the real Socrates, who happened to be in attendance, rose from his seat and stood in silence. In so doing he took an important step in the history of celebrity by fostering, if not intentionally courting, attention.

Socrates may well have come to regret his decision. Some twenty years later he was brought to trial on the charges of not duly acknowledging the gods that the city acknowledged and of corrupting the youth. In the speech he delivered in his defence he claimed that his portrayal in comedy as one 'who busies himself with studying things in the sky and below the earth, and who makes the worse argument into the better' had not only ruined his reputation but also prejudiced the jury irreparably against him.[5]

Aristophanes was not the only comic playwright to present Socrates on stage. The lesser-known Ameipsias did so as well, while three others at least mentioned him in their plays. At his trial Socrates presented himself to the jury as a victim of his own celebrity, though it is important to note that his celebrity status long preceded his characterization in drama.

It says much about celebrity in late fifth-century Athens that a philosopher such as Socrates could feature as the principal character in comedy, even if his *dramatis persona* bore little resemblance to its historical counterpart. Indeed the fact that Socrates was one of the best-known, if hardly one of the best-loved, Athenians of his day testifies to the high profile of philosophers in general. Additional factors contributed to his high visibility. First, he 'hung out', as we would say today, in the agora, conversing in his characteristically acerbic way with anyone who was game enough to tackle him in argument. Secondly, he was of strikingly ugly appearance. Both Plato and Xenophon go so far as to compare him to the snub-nosed satyr Marsyas. All this contributed to his usefulness as a figure of fun in comedy. After all, beauty is a valuable asset in the path to stardom, but so too is its opposite. Lastly, he had an infuriating way of exposing the muddle-headedness of the man in the street. He clearly enjoyed controversy and he never lost an opportunity to denounce the ill-founded opinions of the ignorant and unenlightened majority.

Aristophanes' *Clouds* provides a brilliant insight into the hostility which traditionally-minded Athenians felt towards the new education offered by the sophists – the poet's major target of attack. Unlike his namesake in the play, however, the real Socrates did not run an expensive school for trainee sophists eager to make their mark in the world. Instead he attracted a circle of devoted disciples who were drawn from both extremes of the social spectrum. At the top were prominent aristocrats such as Alcibiades, Critias (a relative of Plato and the leader of the Thirty Tyrants who ruled Athens at the end of the Peloponnesian War), and Charmides (Plato's uncle and one of the Ten who administered the Piraeus under the authority of the Thirty). Alcibiades described the mesmerizing effect which Socrates had upon him as follows: 'Whenever I listen to him my heart beats faster than a Corybant [a kind of Whirling Dervish] … and I see that he has the same effect upon many others.'[6] At the bottom of the social scale were humble men with no intellectual pretensions whatsoever, like Aristodemus, another character in the *Symposium*, who displayed a dog-like devotion to his master.

Socrates' reputation was such that practically every Athenian would have heard of his name. Since he never travelled abroad except on military service, however, he probably wasn't particularly well-known outside Attica, as the anecdote about him rising to his feet during the performance of the *Clouds* indicates. He was, therefore, a very different kind of celebrity from the sophists, even though in many ways he outshone them.

Worthless nobody insults world's most powerful man!

One of the most eccentric gurus that the ancient world produced was a philosopher named Diogenes the Cynic, whom Plato, his contemporary, dubbed a 'mad Socrates'. Diogenes earned the label 'Cynic', which literally means 'dog-like', because of his shameless conduct. Born in the town of Sinope on the south shore of the Black Sea, he was forced into exile in his forties and subsequently divided his life between Athens and Corinth. He rejected convention in favour of the 'natural life', even going so far as to perform his bodily functions in public. He scorned material possessions and satisfied all his needs with the aid of a cloak, a staff, a bowl and a large earthenware pot which served as his home. His outlandish behaviour won many disciples to his ascetic way of life, and made him a very big celebrity.

If Plutarch and others are to be believed, Diogenes' fame even reached the ears of Alexander the Great. Legend has it that the young king became so upset when the philosopher failed to send him a message congratulating him on his coronation that he journeyed to Corinth with the express purpose of making his acquaintance. When he encountered the philosopher stretched out in the sun, Alexander deferentially inquired if there was anything he could do for him. 'Yes,' Diogenes curtly replied. 'Move to one side. You're blocking the sun.'[7] The anecdote indicates just how much a mendicant with a genius for self-promotion was believed capable of achieving in the Greek world.

A handful of Greek philosophers became such celebrities that tyrants and royals sought to avail themselves of their services. Socrates was invited to the court of Archelaus of Macedon (he declined), Plato accepted an invitation from Dionysius I of Syracuse, and Aristotle tutored the young Alexander the Great. Some made their mark in the Roman world too. Among the first were the Stoic philosopher Diogenes, the Peripatetic philosopher Critolaus and the Platonic philosopher Carneades, who came in a delegation to address the Roman Senate in 155 BC. They evidently made a big impact, because Cato the Censor, who publicly vilified all things Greek, advocated their immediate expulsion.

Greek cures Persian king!

The most famous sixth-century BC physician was Democedes of Croton, who acquired expertise in treating injured athletes. Democedes was wooed successively by Aegina, Athens and Samos. His salary rose each time he moved, until Samos came under the control of Persia, whereupon he was thrown into prison. Once the Persian king Darius learnt of his identity, however, he asked him to treat his dislocated ankle. Democedes obliged and went on to cure the king's wife of a breast abscess. He made himself so indispensable to Darius that his request to be released met with constant rebuffs. Eventually he managed to escape to Italy, where, as we saw earlier, he became engaged to Milo's daughter in an effort to prove that he was anything but a nonentity back home. Several other renowned Greek physicians practised medicine at the Persian court, including Apollonides of Cos, Ctesias of Cnidus, and Polycritus of Mende. Though Democedes and Apollonides both owed their appointment to the fact that they were taken prisoner, their reputations, like those of Ctesias and Polycritus, may well have preceded them.

Apart from Hippocrates of Cos, the facts of whose life are completely shrouded in mystery, no ancient physician was more celebrated than Galen of Pergamum (born AD 129). Galen was not only one of the most prolific writers that the ancient world produced but also tireless in the advocacy of his own medical theories. He spent twelve years honing his craft in a variety of cities, including Pergamum, Smyrna, Corinth and Alexandria. After serving as a surgeon in a gladiatorial school in Pergamum – a post ideally suited to the acquisition of hands-on experience in the treatment of wounds and broken bones – he arrived in Rome in AD 162. He quickly won renown by predicting the recovery from fever of the philosopher Eudemus after all other physicians had despaired of his life. He later cured the wife of a prominent senator, again after other distinguished physicians had failed. Like many inveterate attention-seekers, Galen had a talent for stirring up trouble, which made him highly unpopular. In AD 166 he was forced to return to Pergamum, perhaps to avoid being murdered by one of his rivals. He was back in Rome three years later, however, at the request of the Emperor Marcus Aurelius, and remained there till his death. Skill, ambition, assertiveness, the support of influential patrons, a taste for new experiences, plus, all important, a reputation for having made a daring prognosis and a seemingly miraculous cure that flew in the face of conventional wisdom, all combined to rocket Galen to unprecedented medical stardom.

Poet's fishy escape from jaws of death!

It was poets, rather than prose writers, who became celebrities in the ancient world. This is hardly surprising in view of the fact that many of them came from aristocratic families and enjoyed social prestige. Those at the top of their profession charged high fees, were popular in fashionable court circles, and probably enjoyed a measure of political influence.

The first poetic celebrity on record is Arion, who came from the island of Lesbos (late seventh to early sixth century BC). Arion was something of a musical genius, being credited with transforming the dithyramb, a cult song in honour of Dionysus, into a vehicle for avant-garde musical display. On his way back to Corinth from a highly profitable tour of Italy and Sicily, Arion fell into the hands of pirates, eager to fleece him of his fabulous wealth. Just as they were about to throw him overboard, the poet asked if he could sing one last song. The pirates readily agreed, 'overjoyed at the prospect of hearing the world's most famous singer', as Herodotus relates.[8] Donning his poet's outfit – evidently a rather spectacular affair – Arion sang a jazzy number and then jumped, fully clothed, into the sea. A passing dolphin, evidently charmed by his singing, picked him up and delivered him safe to land.

The most famous poet in the first half of the fifth century BC was Pindar, whose name, as we saw earlier (p. 70 above), became synonymous with success in the games. By the second quarter of the fifth century, however, the victory poem had fallen out of fashion. In its place, the work of the Athenian tragedians had begun to attract international attention. The first to receive an invitation to work abroad was Aeschylus, who in 476 BC was invited to Syracuse by the tyrant Hieron I to write a play commemorating the city's foundation. A few years later he returned to Syracuse, this time to revive his tragedy called the *Persians*. His reputation in the neighbouring town of Gela was so high that when he died he was buried there at public expense. It is interesting to note, however, that his epitaph makes no mention of his work as a tragedian. It would be fascinating to know whether this reflects his own preference, and, if so, whether he was equally self-effacing during his life.

Euripides, who features as a character in no fewer than three of Aristophanes' comedies, produced at least two of his plays abroad. In addition, the city of Magnesia in Thessaly granted him honorary citizenship and exemption from taxes. Towards the end of his life he received an invitation to reside permanently at the court of Archelaus of Macedon. He accepted, partly perhaps out of frustration from the somewhat hostile reception that his plays had received in Athens. It is safe to say, however, that by the time of his death Euripides had achieved greater fame than any other playwright before him, though he was hardly a celebrity in the modern sense of the term. Sophocles, who was the most consistently successful tragedian in the poetic competitions, never took up a commission abroad, and, for all we know, was never invited to do so.

The only Greek prose writer who is reported to have acquired a celebrity of sorts is the historian Herodotus. Herodotus, whose status evidently owed something to the nationalistic tone of his work, read extracts from his account of the Persian Wars both in Athens and at the Olympic Games. Report has it that people in the street would point to him and say, 'There is the great Herodotus, who wrote about the Persian Wars in the Ionic dialect and celebrated our victories.'[9]

Fans hound reclusive poet!

In the Roman era it was still the poets who were drawing the crowds, mainly because prose writers did not have an opportunity to read their works in public. We hear of a Greek epigrammatist named Aulus

Licinius Archias, who was famous for being able to improvise on any subject under the sun. Archias toured extensively through Greece, Asia and southern Italy, and provoked something akin to Beatlemania among his fans. The poets continued to win fame and fortune in later antiquity, principally by composing panegyrics and epics, which they recited to large and enthusiastic audiences. One of the most distinguished of these was Claudian, who in *c.* AD 394 gravitated from Upper Egypt to Rome, where he became court poet under the Emperor Honorius.

Curiously, the only Roman poet who, to our best knowledge, was mobbed by his fans was the ultra-shy Vergil. His biographer Suetonius wrote, 'If ever Vergil was recognized in Rome, which he visited very rarely, he would hide in the nearest building to get away from the people who were trailing after him and pointing him out.'[10] Quite possibly the anecdote was inspired precisely by the fact that the poet was notoriously retiring.

Nothing demonstrates more poignantly that prose writers came a distant second to poets than the enormous pleasure which Pliny the Younger derived from being identified as a leading prose writer of his generation (p. 6 above). Pliny's doting (or perhaps long-suffering) wife was the president of his fan club. As he smugly confided in a letter to his aunt, 'She has copies of my books, reads them over and over again, and even learns them by heart.'[11]

St Augustine, author of the first confessional autobiography, went to considerable pains to ensure that his reputation spread as far as possible. He did this by cultivating friendships with established writers such as Paulinus of Nola, who introduced him to a wider literary public beyond his home base in North Africa.[12]

Anonymous masterpiece!

Although the Greeks placed the arts under the divine patronage of Hephaestus and Athena, artists themselves were not associated with a muse, which was an indication perhaps of their essentially artisan status. There is, moreover, nothing equivalent to Giorgio Vasari's *Life of Michelangelo* nor indeed any monograph that deals exclusively with the lives of artists. Even the greatest Greek sculptors are little more than names to us. One of the few exceptions is Pheidias, about whom a number of colourful anecdotes are preserved, including the fact that after completing work on the chryselephantine statue of Athena that stood in the Parthenon he was exiled from Athens on a charge of embezzlement. Another is Praxiteles, who according to Pliny the Elder owed his fame partly to a young man's insane infatuation with his Cnidian Aphrodite, and partly to the fact that King Nicomedes of Bithynia offered to pay a vast sum of money for it (see p. 118 below). In addition, one or two artists turned their hands to writing, such as the sculptor Polyclitus, active in the second half of the fifth century BC, who wrote a treatise called the *Canon* to elucidate the principles of his art. But though we hear of extravagant prices being paid for some works of art, it is by no means clear that artists themselves were high-earners.

The Romans were even more disparaging of artists than the Greeks. Pliny the Elder describes painting as an unsuitable occupation for decent men, while Plutarch claims that no Roman youth of good breeding would ever wish to become a Pheidias or a Praxiteles (or for that matter a lyric poet).[13] In a famous passage of national self-definition Vergil suggests that the Romans, unlike the Greeks, don't 'do' art. Instead they run the world.[14] It wasn't true, of course, as the vast quantity of work that they produced in a variety of media amply proves. Though we don't know how many Romans would have endorsed the opinion that artistic endeavour was an un-Roman activity, it is an interesting fact that some outstanding works of art and architecture, including the Pantheon, were conceived by artists whose names have not come down to us.

The low profile of artists in the Roman world may not be unconnected with what the German literary critic and philosopher Walter Benjamin once called 'the aura of the original'. Most works of art that the Romans owned were either copies or copies of copies. Amid such proliferation, no cult of the artistic personality could take root. Added to this, when Greek works of art began to arrive in Rome in the form of war booty from 211 BC following the sack of Syracuse, contemporary artists became overshadowed by their Greek predecessors. For this same reason the thoroughly modern concept of the artist who is the object of self-directed fascination has no parallel in antiquity and very few artists are known to have painted or sculpted a self-portrait.

Probably the first to attempt a self-portrait was Apelles, the court painter of both Philip II and Alexander the Great.

Teacher justifies savage beatings!

The Romans regarded the teaching profession so highly that a number of its practitioners achieved a celebrity of sorts. Suetonius even composed a short treatise containing thumbnail sketches of their lives. Probably the most famous teacher of all was Lucius Orbilius Pupillus, who, after a successful career in the army, migrated to Rome from Beneventum (modern Benevento in southern Italy) at the advanced age of fifty. It is not clear what prompted him to begin teaching at a time of life when most Romans would have been content to play with their grandchildren. It seems likely, however, that he drew upon his previous experience, for he acquired a reputation for enforcing strict discipline, as Horace, who studied epic poetry under him, testifies. Orbilius even published a work entitled 'On Folly', in which he complained about 'the insults and injuries which teachers endured at the hands of the negligent or ambitious parents of their students'.[15] Though he never became wealthy, his fellow-citizens erected a statue in his honour on their capitol in Beneventum.

Philosophical lookalikes ape idols' dress-code!

Probably at no time in history has the celebrity of professors been greater than in the period known as the Second Sophistic (*c.* AD 60-230). Declamations on topics inspired by ancient history such as 'Who was the best fighter at Marathon?' became all the rage and attracted large audiences of highly educated aficionados. The venues for such performances ranged from imperial courts to theatres. We are particularly well-informed about the modus operandi of these sophists because Philostratus, who first coined the term 'Second Sophistic', wrote brief lives of forty of them. As his account indicates, they were idolized by their students, though it should be noted that they often took steps to encourage precisely this kind of response. Hadrian of Tyre, who occupied the chair of rhetoric in Athens, is typical of the group. He wore costly clothing, sported precious gemstones, and arrived to give his declamations in a carriage drawn by horses with silver-mounted bridles. Further to attract attention, he hosted games, symposia and wild beast hunts. Hadrian became such a celebrity in fact that his pupils 'imitated his accent, copied his gait, and adopted his distinctive style of dress'.[16] Many philosophers became highly influential in the political sphere, were engaged as ambassadors, or intervened to quell riots. As Wilmer Wright observed long ago, 'No other type of intellectual could compete with them in popularity.'[17] Even St Augustine was so enamoured of the eloquence of a Syrian orator named Hierius that he dedicated some of his writings to him.[18] (The less discriminating, he points out, evinced this kind of admiration for charioteers, gladiators and actors.)

Afterlife

The reputation of the sophists went into freefall in the early fourth century BC, largely owing to Plato's depiction of them as money-grubbing charlatans, notably in his dialogue *The Sophist*. In later antiquity, they became admired for their attempt to systematize the teaching of rhetoric. Even so, most of their huge output survives only in the form of fragmentary quotations. Gorgias, whose *Encomium to Helen* has come down to us in its entirety, fared the best. Protagoras, the author of at least fifteen treatises, is represented by fewer than ten fragments.

By contrast, the enduring fame of Socrates was due largely to the fact that he was immortalized in the writings of his pupil Plato. In fact if Plato had not been his pupil, Socrates might have been only an obscure footnote to the history of philosophy. In his case, too, however, a hostile tradition surfaced a few years after his death in the form of a lost treatise which purported to be written by his prosecutors.[19] Half a century later the politician Aeschines observed, 'Men of Athens, you executed Socrates the sophist (*sic*) because he was clearly responsible for the education of Critias, one of the Thirty Tyrants' – as if it was an accepted fact that Socrates had been implicated in the overthrow of the democracy.[20] Xenophon's much more informal portrait of Socrates, which he entitled *Memorabilia* or *Memoirs*, became especially influential in the Roman and Byzantine periods. The biography by Diogenes Laertius, written in the early third century AD, preserves a number of anecdotes which, in light of the philosopher's eccentricity, probably derive from his lifetime.

The hostile tradition was still alive in the second century BC. Cato the Censor described Socrates as 'a mighty chatterbox, who attempted to the best of his ability to be his country's tyrant, both by abolishing its customs and by enticing fellow citizens into positions contrary to the law'.[21] This observation, however, probably had as much do with Cato's hostility towards all things Greek, philosophers especially, as it did with Socrates in particular.

In the following century Socrates emerged as the ideal philosopher type, equally admired for his self-control, his abstemiousness, his disdain for wealth, his disregard for worldly pleasures, and his unflinching courage in the face of death. In Cicero's estimation, it was Socrates who 'took the initiative in summoning philosophy down from heaven ... and in forcing people to ask questions about their lives, about their morals, and about good and evil.'[22] In the estimation of Valerius Maximus he was 'life's best teacher'.[23] Pliny the Elder expressed surprise that it was Pythagoras, rather than Socrates, who had been honoured with a statue in the Roman Forum (see p. 102). Plutarch, who was something of a philosopher himself, wrote treatises entitled 'On the Divine Socrates' and 'On the Condemnation of Socrates'. Marcus Cornelius Fronto, tutor to Marcus Aurelius, revered Socrates as 'that prince of wisdom and eloquence alike'.[24] For Justin, a Christian apologist who died a martyr in Rome in AD 165, he was the forerunner of Jesus. The Neoplatonists, who dominated philosophical thinking from the third to the sixth centuries AD, venerated his memory and celebrated his birthday with sacrifices and speeches in his honour.

Socrates is one of the earliest Greeks whose likeness has come down to us. Report has it that the Athenians felt such remorse after putting him to death that they commissioned a bronze statue by Lysippus (the sculptor who made the official portrait of Alexander the Great in this medium), perhaps around 330 BC, though the earliest surviving portrait, which shows him in the guise of Silenus, was probably made ten or twenty years after his death. Numerous later portraits in the form of heads in the round, statuettes, reliefs, and engravings on gemstones testify to his fame in late antiquity.

The Athenians had such high regard for Pindar that they erected a statue of him in their agora shortly after his death. Alexander the Great spared Pindar's house when he destroyed Thebes out of deference to his poetic accomplishments. Aeschylus' portrait was included in the painting of the battle of Marathon that was displayed in the Painted Stoa in Athens. His monument in Gela in Sicily became a shrine for all those who made their living by performing tragedy. Sometime before 425 BC the Athenians passed a decree permitting 'anyone who wished' to revive his plays at the City Dionysia. A portrait of Sophocles by Polygnotus, which was also displayed in the Painted Stoa, showed the poet in the company of Melpomene, the muse of tragedy, and Asclepius, the healing god. There is also a tradition that he was venerated posthumously as the hero Dexion ('Receiver'). From the fourth century BC onwards Euripides' plays became extremely popular throughout the Greek world and were repeatedly chosen for revival at the City Dionysia. The tyrant Jason of Pherae was so overcome by a performance of *Trojan Women* that he had to leave the theatre before its conclusion. The orator Isocrates died declaiming Euripides' verse. At his last banquet Alexander the Great recited from memory a speech from Euripides' lost play *Andromeda*. In the 330s BC bronze statues of all three tragedians were set up in the theatre of Dionysus in Athens. The three also became the subject of biographies. Though much of the information contained in these works was culled from their plays, the lives of the playwrights may well have begun to excite the interest of the theatre-going public during their lifetimes.[25]

Though he continued to be widely read in antiquity, Herodotus acquired a reputation for being a liar – a viewpoint put forward by Plutarch in a vitriolic essay entitled 'On the Malice of Herodotus'. Plutarch's hostility was, however, based largely on the fact that the historian was less than flattering to his Theban compatriots in his account of the Persian Wars. In the opinion of Aulus Gellius he was, quite simply, 'the most famous writer of history'.[26]

The seal was set on Vergil's immortality by Augustus' decision to override the poet's death-bed request that the *Aeneid* be burnt. The early third-century church father Tertullian identified Vergil as 'a Christian soul by nature' – a status he retained into the late Middle Ages. Around the same time there arose the practice of seeking advice and knowledge about the future by randomly selecting a passage from the *Aeneid*, a type of bibliomancy known as *sortes Vergilianae*.

7

The Religious Charismatic

> If I do not return to the pulpit this weekend, millions of people
> will go to hell.
>
> Jimmy Swaggart, TV evangelist

Fastidious attentiveness to the details and vagaries of cultic performance was the primary qualification for religious office in the ancient
world, since the efficaciousness of any devotional act – whether this
took the form of a prayer, a sacrifice, a votive offering or a festival –
depended largely on the punctiliousness of the undertaking. It follows
that Greek and Roman religion afforded limited opportunities for the
expression of charismatic religious leadership, which the sociologist
Max Weber (1963, 295) defined as 'a rule over men, whether predominantly external or predominantly internal, to which they submit
because of their belief in the extraordinary quality of the specific
person'.

At the margins of the religious establishment, however, the opportunities for such leadership abounded. Polytheism is by definition a
highly competitive system of belief, consisting as it does of a plurality
of cults in constant competition for limited resources. New cults and
movements constantly came into being, while older, less fashionable
ones faded into obscurity. In antiquity these depended for their sur-
vival on the appeal of charismatic religious virtuosi, just as in recent
times Methodism, Mormonism and the Unification Church of Rev.
Moon have done.[1]

Charismatics present a fascinating substratum of ancient religion,
being peripheral, unregulated and independent. We detect traces of
them in Greece from the late Archaic period onwards, answering to
spiritual needs that were not addressed through the apparatus of
state-organized religion, though probably only a small minority of
their actual number has found its way into the historical record. Early
Christianity enjoyed a highly ambivalent relationship with charismat-

ics. On the one hand, it looked askance at their vulgar displays of attention-seeking, which it regarded as a distraction from the spiritual search for God; on the other, it relied heavily upon their personal assertiveness to spread the Christian message.

Typically those who come under the influence of a charismatic virtuoso no longer respond to rational argument, continue to fulfil their social obligations, or even take into account their own self-interest. Instead they submit to his commands (we are talking exclusively about men exercising this attractive power) because of the extraordinary force of his personality. The demands that the virtuoso places upon his followers are absolute. Though we never hear of any late fifth-century BC charismatic mesmerizing Athenian women in the same way as, say, the god Dionysus, posing as a worshipper, mesmerized the women of Thebes in Euripides' *Bacchae*, far less one who challenged the authority of the state, this does not mean that such figures did not exist. On the contrary, the masterly way in which Euripides explores both their appeal and their danger strongly suggests that they were a recognizable feature of the religious landscape in his day.

'Meat bad for you' claims lifestyle guru!

Leading religious charismatics in the Archaic period include the Cretan seer Epimenides, who made a name for himself by purifying Athens after a sacrilege had been committed on the Acropolis; Aristeas of Proconnesus (an island in the Sea of Marmara), who was said to be capable of appearing in two places at once; and Zalmoxis, of unknown origin, who performed exorcisms, rescued towns from epidemics and offered immortality to his followers. Undoubtedly the most successful by far, however, was Pythagoras, who was born on the island of Samos in *c.* 570 BC and emigrated to Croton in south Italy at about the age of forty, where he founded a sect that bore his name.

Pythagoras must have been an extremely effective public speaker in light of the fact that audiences in excess of two thousand are said to have attended his lectures. Eventually some three hundred young men committed their lives to promoting his revolutionary religious ideas and ascetic way of life. What made Pythagoreanism so different is that it dictated every aspect of daily life, including dress, food and

94

hygiene. Though many sects sought to promote a sense of exclusivity by practising commensality or table-fellowship, their reunions were usually limited to ritual occasions. In contrast to these, Pythagoras and his followers maintained a fully communal existence, based on an elaborate set of rules and prohibitions. In consequence, they excluded themselves from the social life of Croton altogether. Two of the most important of these rules, adherence to which was believed to result in a higher reincarnation in the next life, were vegetarianism and abstinence from beans. The Pythagoreans established such a strong sense of solidarity that in time they came to dominate Crotonian politics, which, we may suspect, became an instrument for the implementation of their master's doctrines. Hardly surprisingly, this led to group isolation. Such an outcome can only have been achieved by a highly charismatic leader. Eventually, a violent backlash resulted in the wide-scale slaughter of many of their members, though whether this occurred during Pythagoras' lifetime is unclear.

Although the source of Pythagoras' extraordinary appeal is largely hidden from us, it may be, as Erwin Rohde eloquently put it, that his personality 'became a centre to which a whole community was attracted by a sort of inward necessity'.[2] Ancient authors speak mainly of his physical attributes. His biographer Porphyry, citing a pupil of Aristotle, speaks of his noble and handsome appearance, and the charm of his voice and manner.[3] Attributes such as these are standard in descriptions of religious charismatics, however, and they should probably be interpreted as nothing more than intelligent guesswork. Pythagoras was also reputed to have a golden thigh, the gift of prophecy, and the ability to be in two places at once. It seems safe to infer that he marketed himself as what we would call today a lifestyle guru, that is to say, both as a teacher of religion and as the promoter of a distinctive way of life, and that this potent combination dictated to his disciples how they should conduct themselves both in private and in public.

The ultimate measure of Pythagoras' success lies in the fact that he was able to attract adherents who were prepared to die defending his system of belief. He must have possessed formidable organizational skills, an unshakeable conviction of his own spiritual uniqueness, a visionary belief in a unified religious doctrine which not only required absolute obedience from his followers but also put them at odds with the rest of society, and finally, a keen eye for exploiting political circumstances for his own personal advantage.

Carpenter's son raises roof in Galilee!

John Lennon once got into trouble by boasting that the Beatles were more famous than Jesus Christ. In terms of celebrity, however, he was of course dead right. The carpenter's son (or carpenter *tout court*) from Nazareth does not rate an entry in the *Oxford Classical Dictionary* (3rd edn), which signifies that his impact on the Roman world during his lifetime was almost zero. His fame, though growing at the time of his death, was largely limited to the shores of Lake Galilee, to which his ministry had been confined. No superstar he, but a charismatic of the first order, and the supreme representative of a type of mystic whom we encounter in large numbers in Roman-occupied Judaea.

The Gospels are wholly reticent about the qualities which Jesus identified in his disciples, as they are about the arguments which he used to persuade them to abandon their family ties. Of Simon, Andrew, James and John, we are told simply that he 'called' them and that they 'followed'. As all four were fishermen, they were presumably uneducated. The lowly social status of all twelve disciples contributes considerably to the mystery surrounding the success of the so-called Jesus movement that sprung up after his death.

When his mission had begun to gather momentum, Jesus is said to have appointed 'the seventy', whom he divided into pairs with instructions to precede him 'into every town or place where he himself was about to come'[4]. Crudely put, this sounds very much like a tightly orchestrated publicity campaign, whose goal was to drum up interest in the audience prior to the main event. In fact Jesus and his disciples must have been quite a road show, slogging around the shores of Lake Galilee on foot accompanied by numerous hangers-on, many of whom were unattached women.

The Gospels are equally reticent about Jesus' objectives. The fact that he preached in synagogues at the beginning of his career suggests that his message was not antithetical to mainstream Judaism, even though he stirred up so much animosity when he came to his home town that he barely escaped with his life. Later, as his popularity (and notoriety) grew, he favoured open-air venues. On more than one occasion he attracted large crowds (in the thousands, if the Gospels are to be believed), and it seems likely that the size of his following was increasing towards the end of his life. He specially appealed to the dregs of society, partly because he offered an apocalyptic vision of the end of the world and partly because he was capable of healing diseases and infirmities, including severe psychological disorders. Interestingly, he seems to have made efforts to suppress the reporting of his miraculous healing, which suggests that, like Alexander the Great, he wanted to delimit the terms of his own celebrity.

The Jesus of the Gospels is dogged by the ultra-conservative Pharisees, ever eager for him to let slip some seditious remark that they can relay to the Roman authorities. However, the prominence of this group and the highly negative light in which they are cast may well be an anachronistic reflection of their hostility to the fast-growing Jesus movement at the time when the Gospels were being written. They certainly serve as a useful dramatic foil, in that their punctilious insistence upon the letter of the law epitomizes the exact antithesis to Jesus' message of love and forgiveness. In actual fact, an account of Jesus' life written by a Pharisee might not have read much differently from Lucian's vitriolic biography of the 'false prophet' Alexander of Abonuteichos (see pp. 98-100 below).

Jesus' fatal decision to enter Jerusalem at the season of Passover was a calculated gamble that directly pitched him against the Jewish priesthood. Given the intensity of religious feeling generated by this festival of liberation, the stakes could not have been higher – and so it proved. It was, however, the logical step for a teacher whose mission could no longer be confined to the shores of Lake Galilee. Jesus may well have realized that he was risking his life, though whether he foresaw his own death quite so explicitly as the Gospels suggest is rather doubtful. When he entered the city, an enthusiastic crowd of supporters hailed him as their Messiah. Oddly, there is no evidence to suggest that the disturbance which his arrival caused on the streets of Jerusalem gave rise to any concern among the Roman authorities. Instead it was the Jewish Sanhedrin who instigated his arrest – a clear indication that his mission had made relatively little impact upon non-Jews.

It is easy to overlook how deeply the cultural and social roots of Christianity were embedded in the Graeco-Roman world. Clearly the

Gospel writers were aware of the aretalogical tradition and to some extent modelled their accounts of Jesus' life on pre-existing works in that genre. It is also interesting to speculate whether Jesus himself was aware of the ideal of the Greek sage and whether it influenced the style of his mission.[5] As a charismatic he was by no means unique and his ministry was not atypical of the *modus operandi* of many other religious virtuosi in the first century AD. Another such was Simon Magus, who is described by his followers in Acts as 'that power from God which is called Great'. When Simon saw the apostle Peter giving the Holy Spirit to the people of Jerusalem, he offered him money to reveal the secret of his power, since he was eager to enhance his standing as a virtuoso.[6]

Jesus' widespread appeal was due in part to the multiplicity of roles that he assumed in the course of his ministry – faith-healer, miracle-worker, Messiah, prophet and reforming preacher. It is likely, too, that at least some of his followers interpreted his apocalyptic utterances about the imminent arrival of the Kingdom of God as a direct challenge to Roman authority and saw him as a political revolutionary, even though the Gospels scrupulously avoid any such intention on his part.[7]

Charisma alone would hardly have been enough to enable a man of little if any social distinction or education to become the posthumous inspiration for a new religion. Jesus must have possessed colossal willpower, formidable intelligence, extraordinary powers of leadership, boundless energy, and great reserves of courage. Like the other charismatics we have been examining, he required unconditional devotion from his disciples and warned them that they might have to pay for their devotion with their lives.[8] Such were the force of his personality and the strength of their faith that they followed him undeterred. His impact is all the more astounding in light of the fact that some contemporary scholars now believe that his ministry lasted less than a year.

Pseudo-seer speaks through snake's head!

Polytheism still afforded an open field for religious innovators with a flair for self-promotion well into the centuries that followed the birth of Christ. One of the most successful was Alexander of Abonuteichos, who was comprehensively rubbished as a 'pseudo-seer' by his biographer Lucian of Samosata (modern Samsat in Turkey). Alexander founded a lucrative oracular shrine on the southern coast of the Black Sea in the second half of the second century AD. The shrine took its cue from an alleged epiphany of the healing god Asclepius in the form of a human-headed snake called Glycon.

Lucian makes it his task to expose Alexander's cynical manipulation of the credulous multitude, which the latter masked beneath a superficial veneer of spirituality. He characterizes the charismatic as 'equally adept in lying, guile, perjury, malice, plausibility, audaciousness, cunning, determination, con-artistry and hypocrisy'.[9] He claims that Alexander tried to murder him and admits in turn that he would have cheerfully watched the seer being torn to pieces by foxes and apes. (*Faute de mieux* Lucian took a bite out of Alexander's hand when the latter extended it for him to kiss.) Despite his vitriolic hatred of the seer, however, Lucian does not downplay his enormous popularity. On the contrary, he uses it to mock the pitiful depths of human ignorance. He claims that when Alexander first introduced his god into Abonuteichos in the form of a recently hatched snake 'almost all the inhabitants, including women, old men and boys, came running up to marvel, pray and make obeisance'.[10] He tells us that the cult held a special appeal for Paphlagonians of what he disparagingly calls 'the fat and ignorant' variety.

Within a remarkably short space of time the fame of the oracle had spread throughout the Black Sea region and was making its way to Rome, where it gained the ear of the Emperor Marcus Aurelius. Though Lucian ascribes Alexander's success to the activities of a sinister band of 'fellow conspirators', he does not explain how they differed from any other loyal band of disciples. Alexander offered a kind of comprehensive religious package deal that answered to all the spiritual and material needs of the period. His shrine gave out oracular pronouncements, supervised magical healing in the name of Asclepius, and celebrated mysteries that promised blessedness to initiates in the hereafter. All this was larded over with the precepts of Pythagoreanism, the philosophical school in which the seer himself claimed to have been trained.

Irrespective of whether Alexander was indeed the out-and-out fraud that his biographer suggests, his career provides a textbook of

'How to become a highly-successful charismatic'. Not the least of his assets was his striking appearance, which Lucian concedes was 'god-like'. He also tells us that Alexander was tall and handsome, possessed eyes that shone with religious fervour, and had a mellifluous voice – qualities, incidentally, not unlike those attributed to Pythagoras. He was given to seizures causing his mouth to fill with saliva that was deemed by his supporters to be divine – the ancient equivalent perhaps of ectoplasm.

Alexander's success tells us as much about the spiritual hunger of the age in which he lived as it does about celebrity *per se*. It was greatly to his advantage that he established his oracle in a region that had few competitors, since the proceeds which accrued to it brought considerable economic and political benefit to the local population. In due course Alexander successfully petitioned Marcus Aurelius for permission to change the barbaric-sounding name of the town to Ionopolis and thus to endow it with the status of a Greek city-state. His celebrity was further enhanced by the minting of coins depicting Glycon on the obverse and his head on the reverse.

Crazy squats on pillar for forty years!

Arguably the most extraordinary charismatics that the Early Church produced were the stylite saints (from the Greek word '*stulos*', meaning 'pillar'). They were so-named because they lived their lives perched on tops of columns in the north Syrian desert. The originator of the movement, Simeon the Elder (*c.* 390-459), began his working life as a shepherd boy before becoming an anchorite. The austerity he practised was so extreme, however, that his fellow monks judged him to be wholly unfit for communal living. As a result, he withdrew to the edge of the desert where he lived in a hut for several years.[11]

At about the age of thirty Simeon took up residence on a limestone ridge less than twenty yards in diameter on a hilltop called Telneshe to the east of Antioch. He remained there for the rest of his life – some thirty-six years in all. He ate and slept very little, devoting most of his waking hours to prayer. To escape from the hordes of visitors who came to consult or merely to ogle him, Simeon constructed a small pillar with a platform on top. Originally the pillar was only a few feet in height but over time he increased it to nearly sixty feet.

Though Simeon never offered any explanation for his bizarre form of existence, his elevation was probably intended to be symbolic of his estrangement and aloofness from earthly existence. Theodoret, bishop of Cyrrhus, who visited him in the desert and later wrote an account of his life, tells us that the stylite wore a heavy chain and 'bent his body so low [when he prayed] that his forehead almost touched his feet'.

Not surprisingly, Simeon's highly idiosyncratic behaviour resulted in his becoming a huge celebrity and his pillar became a focus of popular pilgrimage. As Theodoret reports:

> As they all come from every quarter, each road is like a river: one can see collected in that spot a human sea into which rivers from all sides debouched. For it is not only inhabitants of our part of the world who pour in, but also Ishmaelites, Persians and the Armenians subject to them, the Iberians, the Homerites, and those who live further in the interior than these. Many came from the extreme west: Spaniards, Britons and the Gauls who dwell between them. It is superfluous to speak of Italy (tr. R. Doran [1992, 19]).

Far from withdrawing from human intercourse, however, Simeon devoted several hours of each day to conversing with the many suppliants who came to seek the benefit of his spiritual wisdom. In addition, community leaders sought his advice on how to deal with epidemics. He also engaged in correspondence and gave instruction to his disciples. His renown was such that when the Emperor Theodosius learnt that he had injured his foot, he hastily dispatched to him three bishops, who urged the saint to abandon his pillar and receive medical attention. True to form, Simeon left his cure in the hands of God and recovered soon afterwards. It is difficult to resist the impression that Simeon, as his enemies alleged, deliberately courted his ascetic star status. Quite possibly he thought it consistent with his role as a religious zealot, on the grounds that spirituality has to attain visibility in order to make an impact on society.

One of the ways in which Simeon continued to engross his followers throughout his long and somewhat uneventful life was by progressively dispensing with every vestige of bodily comfort. In his earlier years he attached himself to a stake during Lent so that he could more easily remain upright while fasting, whereas in his later years he maintained this posture unaided. In the final year of his life he is said to have mortified himself yet further – by balancing on one leg.

Afterlife

It was Pythagoras' disciples who initially fostered his posthumous reputation, by continuing to play an important part in the political affairs of southern Italy and Sicily long after his death. In the following century Pythagoras' standing was such that it became *de rigueur* for a religious virtuoso to claim association with him. In the fourth century BC his ideas (or what passed for them in common currency) were incorporated into the philosophical systems of Plato and Aristotle. In Middle Comedy of the fourth century BC the Pythagorean philosopher became a stock figure of ridicule. His own reputation remained high, however, and from the third century BC onwards many forged documents were attributed to him.

Pythagoras was equally revered in the Roman world. In 343 BC his statue was erected in the *comitium* (or place of assembly) in the Roman Forum, out of respect for his exemplary wisdom.[12] Perhaps the greatest testimony to his high reputation is the fact that Rome's second king Numa Pompilius, who was noted for his exceptional wisdom and piety, was alleged to have received instruction from the sage. In the first century BC Pythagoreanism staged a considerable comeback in Rome, largely thanks to the efforts of a scholar and mystic called Publius Nigidius Figulus. In deference to the sage's authority, the polymath Marcus Terentius Varro, one of antiquity's greatest scholars, was buried in leaves of myrtle, olive and black poplar, as was traditional among Pythagoras' sectaries.[13] Ovid assigns him a focal position at the conclusion of his *Metamorphoses* as humankind's first and greatest teacher. Similarly Juvenal concludes his rant against the Egyptians for allegedly practising cannibalism in his *Satire* 15 with a respectful tribute to Pythagoras' vegetarianism. With the rise of Christianity, Pythagoras acquired the status of a kind of pagan saint, even though he was not without his detractors.[14] In the late third and early fourth centuries AD Iamblichus and Porphyry both wrote biographies of him. He was claimed as the author of an influential set of moral precepts known as 'The Golden Words', which served to elevate the moral tone of late paganism.

Though the followers of Jesus were doubtless crushed and demoralized by their master's death, later Christians (how much later we cannot tell) interpreted the crucifixion as the fulfilment of scriptural prophecy. For the first half-century AD there is no reference either to Jesus or to any of his followers in any extant document. The seven surviving letters of the ex-Pharisee Paul, written some time between 50 and the early 60s AD, provide our earliest source, though they contain few references to the historical Jesus. (Paul is mainly interested in the risen Christ and in the relationship between Jesus and God.) The canonical Gospels were all written at least forty years after Jesus' death. Most of the books that comprise the New Testament were composed in the next half-century and were assembled into a collective entity in the second half of the second century AD.

The earliest reference to Jesus in a non-Christian source is found in the *Jewish Antiquities* by the Jewish historian Josephus (mid 90s AD). Though some scholars believe the passage in question to be a Christian forgery, the contemptuous reference to 'a performer of paradoxical feats, a teacher of people who accept the unusual (?) with pleasure, (who) won over many of the Jews and also many Greeks' may well reflect Josephus' own opinion of Jesus.[15] Some twenty years later Tacitus alluded to Christ's death under Pilate in connection with the fire that ravaged Rome in AD 64, which Nero blamed on the Christians.[16] In sum, it is highly likely that most Romans had heard of Jesus' name by the early decades of the second century AD; or at least they had heard the designation '*Christianus*', which was applied pejoratively to his followers.

Though Lucian regarded the death of Alexander of Abonuteichos – in horrible agony, if he is to be believed – as just deserts for his shameless exploitation of the credulous masses, the cult which he founded retained its prominence well into the late third, and possibly even into the fourth century AD. The name 'Ionopolis' survives to this day as modern Inebolu in Turkey.

When Simeon the Stylite died, an altercation broke out between the churches of Antioch and Constantinople for the possession of his body. Antioch eventually won. As the sixth-century church historian Evagrius Scholasticus reports, 'Simeon's holy body ... was escorted by the garrison (at Antioch), with a great concourse guarding the venerable body, to prevent the inhabitants of the neighbouring cities from gathering and carrying it off.'[17] A vast martyrium, known today as Qalat Simân (the house of Simeon), was built near Aleppo in the late fifth century to house his remains at the instigation of the Emperor Zeno. The martyrium has been aptly described as 'the greatest basilica in the Levant' and is surpassed only by Hagia Sophia in Istanbul. The image of the saint was reproduced numerous times, especially in Rome. Simeon inspired many imitators, and stylitism itself remained a popular form of asceticism in Syria until the Muslim conquest in 636.[18]

8

The Showbiz Star

You can't help but change a little bit, but on the inside I'm still
completely the same person.

Britney Spears, pop singer

The showbiz world of antiquity comprised a motley assortment of
rhapsodes, actors, musicians, tightrope walkers, clowns, jugglers,
charioteers and gladiators. Though it may seem improbable that any
of them achieved the iconic status of, say, a modern rock star, some
came very close. Nothing illustrates this better than the fact that the
Emperor Nero desperately sought to be included in their ranks. Not
surprisingly, it was a type of celebrity that offended many sober-
minded citizens, including the early Christians. St Augustine for one
heaped scorn on the adulation that actors received and said that he
'would rather live in obscurity than be known in the way they were
known, and would rather be hated than loved in the way they were
loved'.[1] This, however, sounds very much like sour grapes, as the saint
greatly desired to see his own name in lights.

Since many of the structures that were purpose-built for mass
entertainment were extremely large even by modern standards, audiences should typically be numbered in the thousands, if not in the tens
of thousands. Although they lacked the means to create the peculiarly
intense bond that is today so effortlessly forged between stars and fans
by media saturation, entertainers did their best to milk their larger-
than-life personalities offstage as well as on. As we saw earlier,
chariot-racing became the most popular form of entertainment in the
early Byzantine period. Though showbiz was dominated, at least
initially, by men, female dancers and musicians are already known to
us in the Classical era. It was only in the Imperial period, however,
that women began to achieve a celebrity status comparable to that of
men, notably as mimes.

105

Rhapsodic rapture!

Our earliest glimpse of professional entertainers in the Greek world is provided by Phemius and Demodocus, bards who feature prominently in the *Odyssey*, declaiming hexameter verse to the accompaniment of the lyre in the palaces of their aristocratic hosts. In later times these bards took the title of 'rhapsodes' or song-stitchers, probably because they provided extempore performances at the bidding of their hosts. The most prestigious rhapsodes identified themselves as the Homeridae. They flourished on Chios and, as their name indicates, claimed to be descended from Homer. Rhapsodes were in fact the first entertainers to form themselves into a guild to protect the interests of their members.

From the late sixth century BC onwards rhapsodes began to compete for prizes at public festivals. The apocryphal report of a contest between Homer and Hesiod probably dates to this period. Thus began a tradition of competitive recitation that was to last for nearly a thousand years. Plato's *Ion*, which is named after a rhapsode who came from Ephesus in Asia Minor, is evidence of the immense popularity of these entertainers in the late fifth and early fourth centuries BC. At the beginning of the dialogue Ion explains that he has just arrived in Athens from Epidaurus, where he won first prize in the quadrennial games in honour of the healing god Asclepius. Ion is confident he will be equally successful in the forthcoming Panathenaic Games. Rhapsodes didn't just compete at the major festivals, however. On the contrary, they gave performances at venues throughout the Greek world. Their ubiquitousness is indicated by the claim of one aficionado that he listened to their recitations 'almost every day'.[2]

Rhapsodes were a kind of one-man band. When competing in the games they drew attention to themselves by wearing gold crowns and other elaborate attire, and they delivered their lines standing on a raised daïs. Their performances must have been spellbinding, which is why Socrates took so much exception to them, likening their effect upon their audiences to something akin to Bacchic possession. They were allegedly capable of attracting audiences of over twenty thousand, which puts them on a par with actors.[3] They also gave public lectures on Homer, arguing in support of the pedagogical value of his verse. And like the sophists they were handsomely rewarded for their services, which is yet another reason why Socrates objected to them.

The star is born!

The beginnings of theatrical stardom in Athens may be traced to the year 449 BC when a prize for the best *tragoidos* (tragic actor) was introduced at the festival of the City Dionysia. The Lenaea festival followed suit about seventeen years later. Though we do not know what impact this innovation had upon performance styles, it certainly signals a growing focus upon actors as interpretative artists. The archon eponymous, the magistrate who had the responsibility of deciding which dramas should be performed at the festivals, also had the task of assigning the actors. It would not be surprising if a kind of bidding war for the best actors ensued, though it is also possible that they were allocated by lot. It is important to note, however, that all actors were amateurs in the fifth century, and that none to our best knowledge performed anywhere other than in Athens. Such celebrity as actors achieved, therefore, would have been very limited in scope.

All that changed in 386 BC when a contest in 'old' (i.e. revived) drama was introduced at the City Dionysia. Actors now began to develop individual repertoires based on highlights from classical, i.e. fifth-century, tragedy. By specializing in particular roles they were able to adopt more idiosyncratic acting styles. In time some of them became typecast. Timotheus of Zacynthus, for instance, became famed for his rendition of Ajax's suicide in Sophocles' play of that name. It became, so to speak, his signature tune and was no doubt requested wherever he performed – much as 'My way' was requested by the fans of Frank Sinatra.[4]

In line with their increased reputations, star actors began to develop a cult of personality. Aristotle wrote of an actor called Theodorus that 'he did not allow anyone, even a minor actor, to enter before he did, because the audience grew attached to the voices they heard first'.[5] The same theatrical self-consciousness – one of the hallmarks of celebrity throughout history – is already evident in a famous anecdote that is told about another actor named Polus, who used his recently deceased son's ashes as a kind of stage prop in a scene from Sophocles' *Electra*.[6] The blurring of the distinction between Polus and his *dramatis persona* marks a significant development in theatrical history, signalling as it does that actors had become an object of fascination in their own right.

By the middle of the fourth century BC star actors were held in such high esteem that their services were occasionally employed in delicate international negotiations. Aristodemus and Neoptolemus were both given grants of Athenian citizenship so that they could negotiate on Athens' behalf with Philip II of Macedon. Since Philip was a fan of the theatre, it's highly probable that he at least knew their names, and their fame would surely have guaranteed them an enthusiastic reception at his court. We know for a fact that Philip remunerated them from his private purse, even though he failed to modify his policy towards Athens as a result of their visit.

The Hellenistic period saw a huge growth in the number and size of public spaces dedicated to the display of theatrical talent. It also saw an increase in the number of theatrical competitions held throughout the Greek-speaking world. A preference for solo song over choral lyric further helped to showcase the art of the *tragoidos*. With the exception of royalty, star actors probably became the best-known as well as the best-loved personages of the age. Though the masks that they wore on stage would have made them less recognizable to the public than showbiz personalities today, their entourage of fans somewhat compensated for this fact.

A clear indication of growing public interest in actors is their increasing popularity in art. A striking example is provided by a wall-painting from Pompeii that is thought to derive from a Greek original dated *c.* 300 BC. It depicts a handsome young tragic actor who is dedicating his mask at a shrine, presumably after having just won a victory in a dramatic contest.[7] Tacitus, writing in the second century AD, speaks of the thunderous applause that greeted even ordinary actors when they struck a pose on stage, and in all probability this was a feature of theatrical performances in earlier times as well.[8]

Since many theatrical contests offered lucrative cash rewards, itinerant actors could now become full-time professionals. A few amassed large fortunes, were courted by royalty, and – a true measure of their celebrity status – had their portraits painted by leading artists of the day. We don't know exactly what the earnings of those at the top amounted to, but some actors became extremely wealthy. The Athenian *tragoidos* Theodorus donated seventy drachmas to the re-building of the temple of Apollo at Delphi in 362 AD – nearly five times as much as any other private donor. Though the report that Aristodemus (or, according to another source, Polus) was paid a talent for a single performance in a competition – a vast sum of money by the standards of the day – is almost certainly an exaggeration, a star actor might well have received as much for a single performance as a skilled labourer would expect to earn in a year.[9]

The formation of guilds called 'the artists of Dionysus' (*hoi peri ton Dionyson technitai*) in the early third century BC consolidated the status of theatrical entertainers. These guilds, which ultimately spread throughout the entire Greek-speaking world, negotiated the terms under which their members appeared at civic festivals by arranging contracts, securing exemptions from taxation and military service on their behalf, and guaranteeing their freedom of movement. In the Roman world the guilds acquired imperial patronage, and they remained an effective lobby until late antiquity.

In the course of time other developments boosted the celebrity of Greek actors. First, in recognition of their unrivalled expertise, stars were accorded the privilege of appearing in contests without any competitors. Secondly, they were invited to give public performances during but outside the structure of the civic festival. Thirdly, cities vied with one another in granting them such honours as status of guest-friend and public benefactor, freedom from arrest, and the privilege of a front seat in the theatre.

Actors also became the focus of gossip – a sure sign that their lives had begun to acquire something of the aura of modern celebrities. Photius, the ninth-century AD author of a *Lexicon*, quotes excerpts from a work by a certain Rufus of unknown date who narrated 'the various escapades of both tragic and comic actors, the celebrity of musical composers and performers, together with revelations about whom they had affairs with and which of them were friends of kings'. Showbiz gossip had entered the western tradition.

No second fiddle for our musicians!

In the Greek world percussion instruments, including castanets, cymbals and hand-held drums, were largely confined to revelry and cult.

In fact the only instruments that were played in front of large audiences were the lyre (Greek, *kithara*; Latin, *cithara*) and the pipe (Greek, *aulos*; Latin, *tibia*). Though pipers seem to have achieved more visibility in the Greek world overall, in Athens at least lyre-players enjoyed greater prestige. This was largely due to the fact that many *aulos*-players were of either servile or foreign extraction, though Alcibiades' contemptuous dismissal of the instrument as unbecoming to a free man didn't help matters either (see p. 18f. above).

Midas of Acragas, who won the crown for *aulos*-playing at the Pythian Games in *c.* 490 BC, may have been slave-born. Midas was the only non-aristocrat to commission a victory ode from Pindar, a fact which tells us much both about his desire for celebrity and about the wealth that he must have acquired. (His is also the only ode that Pindar wrote for the victor of a non-athletic or non-equestrian event.) The most famous pipe-player of all time was a Theban named Pronomos, who is depicted on an Attic mixing bowl of late fifth-century date. The elaborately attired musician is seated in the centre of the composition, surrounded by the cast of a satyr play (the dramatic coda to a tragic trilogy). The most famed lyre player of this era was an Athenian named Arignotus, whose celebrity was such according to the Chorus in Aristophanes' *Knights* that he was 'known to all'. Arignotus also happens to be one of the very few historical characters whom Aristophanes mentions by name without disparaging his character.[10]

Musicians were also available for private hire. An *aulêtês* named Euius of Chalcis was invited by Alexander the Great to play at his wedding at Susa in 324 BC. We hear of another pipe-player who was paid two thousand four hundred drachmas for a single performance.[11] As has been the case throughout history, rates of pay were probably commensurate with reputations. There were no competitions for female musicians, so virtually the only outlet for their talent was the symposium, at which they would be expected to provide sexual favours as well. In fact two of the most famous pipe-players were the courtesans Lamia and Nanno.[12]

No names of any celebrity musicians have come down to us from the Roman era, due both to the deep-seated prejudice regarding their lowly origins and to the relatively low esteem in which musical talent was held.

Dictator hobnobs with actors!

Though actors were also regarded with disdain by the Romans, some of them achieved considerable celebrity. The contempt which accompanied them in official circles is indicated by the fact that the manager of a theatrical troupe was sometimes referred to as the *dominus gregis* or 'master of the herd'. Privately, however, they were highly valued, as we see from the fact that when Caesar's assassin, Marcus Brutus, sought to acquire the services of a well-known Greek actor called Canutius, he appealed to the latter's friends to intervene on his behalf, because, in his words, 'no Greek could properly be required to appear'.[13]

The most famous actor to tread the boards in ancient Rome was the comic actor Quintus Roscius Gallus. A slave by birth, Roscius was elevated to the rank of knight by his close friend and fan, the dictator Sulla. He was also on intimate terms with Cicero, who successfully defended him against the charge of fraudulent business dealings. In order, as it seems, to invite comparison between himself and Hercules, Roscius claimed that in infancy he had been embraced by a snake. He is said to have earned five hundred thousand sesterces a year.[14] When he died Cicero wrote, 'Who is so uncultivated or insensitive as to be unaffected by Roscius' death?' Sulla fraternized with several other theatrical personalities, including a mime called Sorex and a female impersonator called Metrobius. He actually preferred Metrobius' company to that of his wife and contracted a deadly venereal infection from him.[15]

Over the course of time a number of laws were passed that were intended to discourage members of the élite from joining the profession on the grounds that it fostered *licentia* or disorderliness among its practitioners. In AD 15, under the Emperor Tiberius, the Senate even went so far as to debate whether to pass a law allowing praetors to use the lash on actors as a means of quelling the unrest.[16] A senatorial decree passed in AD 19, whose text is preserved in a fragmentary inscription which came to light in Larinum (modern Larino in southern Italy), imposed severe penalties on senators and equestrians who appeared either on stage or in the gladiatorial arena in defiance of a pre-existing ban.[17]

It wasn't just the disorderliness of the actors that gave the authorities a headache, however. The rivalries between their fans were so acute that they sometimes resulted in riots. Eventually in AD 212 the

Emperor Caracalla decreed that all Roman citizens who entered the profession would be categorized as *infames* (i.e. without honour) and incur stiff legal disabilities. Whether this measure proved a more effective disincentive than any of its predecessors is doubtful. Notoriety, after all, runs a close second to celebrity.

Stripper on stage!

Following the death of Roscius, drama ceased to have a strong hold over the Roman public and we never again hear of theatrical stars of comparable brilliance. It was supplanted by two new forms of entertainment called mime and pantomime, both of which were destined to have a very long life.[18] Mime, which could be accompanied by singing, dancing or music, was performed with or without masks. Any subject could inspire it, including folklore and tales from real-life. It was often erotic and sometimes lewd. Mime was performed in theatres, amphitheatres and even hippodromes, all of which indicates that it attracted very large audiences. The artists were extremely well paid, as we see from a law dated to the late fourth century AD, which limited the wearing of luxurious clothing by female mimes.

The most distinguished artists had access to the imperial court. We hear of one named Mnester, who was the lover first of Poppaea Sabina, the mother of Nero's wife Poppaea, and later of Claudius' wife Messalina; and of another named Halityrus, who had sufficient clout to secure an interview with Caligula on behalf of an embassy from Judaea. A certain Bassilla, whose funerary stele was erected in *c.* AD 220 in the amphitheatre in Aquileia on the Adriatic coast, was commemorated for having 'won resounding fame among many peoples and many cities for her excellence among mimes'.[19] The most famous artiste of all was the Empress Theodora, whose extraordinary career will be examined in the final chapter.

Pantomime was in general a more refined artistic medium than mime. Here a mute solo dancer mimed all the characters of a story to a musical accompaniment. Though the pantomime artist was sometimes accompanied either by a chorus or by a soloist, gestures and movements were his (or her) only means of communication. The story was usually drawn from mythology. Tradition has it that pantomime was introduced into Rome in the reign of Augustus by an Alexandrian named Bathyllus and a Cilician named Pylades. In all likelihood, however, it had already begun making headway in the capital a generation earlier. Under Augustus, it became all the rage. The most famous pantomime artist of his day, if not the most famous of all time, was the aforementioned Pylades, as we see from the fact that at least five other artists called themselves Pylades in the course of the next two centuries, hoping to emulate his popularity. Another famous artist was Paris, who enjoyed the confidence and favour of the Emperor Nero until the latter put him to death, possibly out of jealousy of his celebrity.

During the reign of Tiberius the fans of pantomime artists became so unruly that the emperor saw fit to introduce legislation to curb their excesses.[20] Henceforth senators were not permitted to enter the houses of pantomime artists and knights were debarred from mobbing them when they appeared in public. It's noteworthy that this legislation was directed towards members of the élite. Lower-class Romans are unlikely to have been less effusive. Though the Christian Church regularly railed against its alleged 'offensiveness', pantomime did not finally disappear until the time of the Arab conquest. Predictably its practitioners won the hearts of their fans. The epitaph of a certain Vincentius (early third century AD), who came from Thamugadi (Timgad) in modern Algeria, describes him as 'the glory of pantomime artists, living forever on the lips of the public'.[21]

Spectators kill for seats!

Practically the only way for someone from the absolute dregs of society to achieve celebrity status in the Roman world was by becoming a gladiator. Though the gladiatorial profession, if it can be properly called that, chiefly comprised convicted murderers, slaves, arsonists and other low-life characters, such was its glamour that freeborn women, knights, senators and even the Emperor Commodus eventually queued up to get a piece of the action. The glamour they craved derived from the fact that gladiators risked their lives for no loftier purpose than the gratification of the crowd. St Augustine's description of the effect that the arena had upon his friend Alypius tells us a great deal about the hold that the spectacle exercised over educated and supposedly refined youths:

As soon as Alypius saw blood he instantly became crazed. He
didn't turn aside his head but fixated upon the spectacle, devouring the Furies themselves in his ignorance. Delighting in the
cruelty of the arena and becoming drunk with bloodthirsty lust,
he was no longer the person he had been when he first arrived
but had become a part of the rabble that had brought him there,
their intimate associate in fact.[22]

Though gladiatorial combat had a long tradition reaching back to
before the middle of the third century BC, it wasn't until the first
century AD that a star system began to gain headway. Pictures of
gladiators were now displayed in public places, advertising forthcoming attractions. The wealthy freedman Trimalchio, who is the leading
figure in Petronius' *Satyricon* (AD *c.* 61), owns drinking cups that are
decorated with scenes from a combat between two famous gladiators
named Hermerus and Petraites. Trimalchio is such a fan of Petraites
that he instructs his stone mason to carve 'all the fights of Petraites'
on his funerary monument.[23] Another celebrity gladiator was Hermes,
'trained to win but not to kill', who is the subject of an epigram by
Martial.[24] The most famous gladiator of all time was, of course, the
Thracian Spartacus, the leader of the slave revolt which terrorized
Italy from 73 to 70 BC. Spartacus won some nine battles against the
Romans and even threatened to attack Rome. Since he broke out of a
gladiatorial school at Capua while still apparently in training, however,
we don't know whether he ever competed in the arena.

Numerous amphitheatres scattered throughout the Empire were
purpose-built for gladiatorial displays. One of the earliest stone structures, with a seating capacity of about fifteen thousand, was erected
at Aosta (Augusta Praetoria Salassorum) in the foothills of the Alps
some time around the end of the first century BC and the beginning of
the first century AD. Less that a century later the Emperor Titus built
the Flavian Amphitheatre, popularly known from the Middle Ages
onwards as the Colosseum, which is estimated to have accommodated
fifty thousand. The peak in the popularity of gladiatorial combat
occurred in the reign of the Emperor Trajan, who in AD 107 sponsored
a hundred and twenty-three days of celebrations throughout the
Empire, including games at Rome featuring five thousand pairs of
gladiators and ten thousand beasts, to celebrate the success of his

campaign against the Dacians, a people who lived in the loop of the lower Danube.

Like bullfighters, their cultural descendants, gladiators were famed for their sexual potency. Their erotic appeal is the subject of graffiti scrawled on the walls at Pompeii. 'Celadus the Thracian makes all the girls sigh,' says one graffito. 'Crescens the Net-fighter holds the hearts of all the girls,' says another.[25] Further evidence of the fantasies that they inspired lies in the fact that pieces of their clothing were auctioned off to the highest bidder after a contest. In his vicious tirade against women the satirist Juvenal pours scorn upon a senator's wife called Eppia for eloping to Egypt with a gladiator named Sergius. What was the attraction? Juvenal demands. The fellow was a physical wreck. 'Ah, but he was a gladiator. That's what transforms his like into pretty boys. That's what she preferred to children, country, sister and husband. What her sort love is *iron*.'[26] ('*Ferrum*', 'iron', also carries the crude sexual connotation of our word 'prick'.)

Marcus Aurelius' wife Faustina is said to have become completely besotted with a gladiator, and it was even rumoured that the man in question was the father of her son Commodus. The fact that Commodus had allegedly been sired by a gladiator was popularly given as the reason for his fixation upon the arena. Such allegations were, incidentally, part of a familiar Roman complaint about the insatiable sexual appetites of aristocratic women, the gratification of which was seen as a dangerous violation of the social hierarchy (see p. 125 below).

We don't have enough evidence to enable us to make a confident assessment of the death-rate of gladiators. Using graffiti from Pompeii, Mary Beard and Keith Hopkins (2005, 87) have recently suggested that it may have been as high as one in six per fight. From sepulchral inscriptions they further calculate that the average age at death was as low as 22.5 years. Assuming that a gladiator began fighting at about the age of seventeen, most careers would therefore have lasted less than six years. However, other scholars such as David Potter (1999, 315) have suggested that the death-rate was much lower. Certainly those who displayed exceptional skill and bravery are likely to have been spared when they found themselves on the losing end of a fight, and we know for a fact that a number of gladiators were eventually granted their freedom.

It goes without saying that gladiators drawn from the ranks of criminals and slaves enjoyed their celebrity in name only, as they would have been confined to barracks for the majority of their working lives. The true stars were the *auctorati*, free men, that is, who hired themselves out as gladiators on a strictly professional basis. Though they, too, may never have fully overcome the stigma associated with the arena, some of them earned huge sums of money. Suetonius reports that Tiberius paid some retired gladiators a thousand *aurei* apiece to appear in games which were held in memory of his grandfather Drusus, and that Nero provided a gladiator named Spiculus with a palace and estate worthy of someone who had won a triumph.[27] Eventually Marcus Aurelius imposed a ceiling of twelve thousand sesterces on the fees that *auctorati* could charge for a single appearance. Gladiatorial contests continued to be held until the end of the fourth century in the eastern half of the Roman Empire and until the fifth century in the West.

Afterlife

Only a handful of actors seem to have won their way to posthumous celebrity. On the Greek side, the best remembered were Neoptolemus and Polus. They both earned mention in an anthology by Stobaeus (early fifth-century AD?), which, as Pat Easterling (2002, 333) observes, 'guaranteed them canonical status along with many of the most famous people of the Greek world'.[28] Virtually the only Roman actor to be evoked by posterity was Roscius, whose name became synonymous with consummate theatrical skill – a status that it achieved again in eighteenth-century England with the publication of treatises and satires about the acting profession known as 'Rosciads'. Roscius was identified by Aulus Gellius two centuries after his death as 'an actor of consummate grace'.[29]

A dead gladiator cut no mustard, and very few names have come down to us. The most talked-about in later times was Spartacus, whose dreaded memory helped stoke fears among the Romans on the occasion of an attempted break-out from a gladiatorial school at Praeneste (Palestrina) in AD 65.[30] Spartacus was also cited approvingly as an innovative strategist in Frontinus' work on military stratagems, which was published some two decades later.[31]

9

The Sexually Liberated Female

Glamour is what I sell. It's my stock in trade.

Marlene Dietrich, film star

According to Thucydides, Pericles ended his speech commemorating the Athenians who had died in the first year of the Peloponnesian War by paradoxically remarking that 'the highest glory (*kleos*) for a woman is to be spoken of neither in praise nor in blame'.[1] Social invisibility, in other words, was the yardstick of female respectability. The fact that virtually no native-born Athenian woman has entered the historical record indicates that the overwhelming majority did indeed conform – with what degree of compliance we cannot of course know – to Pericles' rigid gender-stereotyping. The same is likely to have been true of most other Greek communities, and the situation was not much different in the Roman world until the last century of the Republic. Denied all but the most basic education because of their 'innate incapacity', excluded from public life other than in the religious sphere, permitted to go abroad only when attended by relatives or slaves, freeborn women rarely enjoyed much prominence.

There were in fact only two categories of women who managed to break the social code: first, those of aristocratic birth, who became adjuncts to powerful males, either as mothers, wives, sisters or daughters; and secondly, those of lowly origin, who became entertainers or prostitutes. An even smaller group of talented women succeeded in making a name for themselves as intellectuals. Overall the percentage of women who achieved celebrity status in the ancient world was therefore minute by comparison with men. Celebrity may be a poor guide to true talent, but its unavailability to half the population would have acted as a colossal brake upon creative talent and original thinking.[2]

117

Ankle-judging contest in Panathenaic Games!

Women's visibility in the contemporary celebrity stakes probably owes more to glamour than to anything else. Glamour, however, like celebrity itself, was something the Greeks didn't have a word for, though *thelxis*, 'seduction', perhaps comes closest. It was virtually impossible to praise a woman for her beauty without impugning her chastity. In the poems of Homer, women are noted for their ankles, their arms and their cheeks, never for their legs, their breasts or their buttocks. When in the *Iliad* the Trojan elders catch sight of the gorgeous Helen on the ramparts, they comment approvingly in general terms about her beauty, but give no hint as to what it consisted in. Similarly in the *Odyssey*, when Odysseus wishes to pay a compliment to the beautiful young princess Nausicaa, he compares her to a laurel tree that he once saw growing on the island of Delos. Even Aphrodite, the goddess of sex and sexual love, is described not as 'ample-bosomed' or 'possessed of juicy thighs' but as 'laughter-loving' and 'golden'.

Though beauty contests for boys and girls featured as events at some athletic contests, everything that we know about Greek society suggests that these would have been extremely prim affairs, with, at most, only the face and ankles of the female contestants exposed to the judges' critical gaze. Certainly nothing of the hoopla that greets the crowning of Miss World would have been accorded, say, to the crowning of Miss (or indeed Mr) Panathenaic Games.

Whereas the nude male had been a socially acceptable subject of monumental sculpture from the late seventh century BC onwards, it wasn't until the Hellenistic period that statues of naked women entered the artistic canon. And when they did, they were to be read, overtly at least, as representations of the goddess Aphrodite rather than of flesh-and-blood women – a situation not unlike that which prevailed in art in modern times until the middle of the nineteenth century. The first-known female nude was commissioned by the inhabitants of the island of Cos from Praxiteles. Pliny the Elder tells us that when the sculptor presented them with his work, the islanders were so shocked that they declined to accept it and ostentatiously ordered a draped version instead.[3] The original was sold off to the neighbouring Cnidians, whose fame shot up accordingly. Such, allegedly, was its erotic power that a man who got accidentally locked up

118

with it overnight inside a temple indecently assaulted it. There is, however, nothing to suggest that either Praxiteles' nude or the many nudes that followed in its wake ushered in an era of more overt sexual self-presentation on the part of Greek women, though it certainly gave voyeurism on the part of Greek males a public outlet for its satisfaction.

Glamour was equally absent in the Roman world. Even in love poetry women are little more than a hazy blur. Lesbia, to whom Catullus dedicated some of the most haunting love poems ever conceived, is a visual blank, and much the same is true of Propertius' Cynthia. Of the Carthaginian queen Dido, one of literature's most memorable creations, Vergil tells us absolutely nothing other than the fact that she was 'golden-haired', and even this tantalizing detail is not vouchsafed to the reader until her death-scene.

High-class hooker's biggest erection!

Apart from showbiz, the only profession that enabled a girl to make a really big name for herself was prostitution. There were two categories of prostitutes: the *pornê* or common prostitute; and the *hetaera* or 'female companion', who, in addition to providing sexual favours, was expected to entertain and converse intelligently with her clients. In practice, however, the distinction was fluid, since many *pornai* graduated to the rank of *hetaerae*. To complicate matters further, both terms were sometimes applied to the same woman. The fact remains, however, that a *hetaera* needed brains as well as beauty in order to be a success in her profession.

The opportunities for fame and enrichment on the part of a talented *hetaera* were virtually limitless. Herodotus tells us, with surely a pinch of hyperbole, that the name of a Thracian *hetaera* called Rhodopis 'became known to every Greek'. Rhodopis amassed such a fortune that she was reputed to have financed the building of one of the pyramids. This was, he points out, an absurd anachronism since she lived in the sixth century BC, many centuries after their construction. Even so, the anecdote still testifies to the extravagant fees that women at the top of their profession were able to charge for their services. A little later, Herodotus claims, another *hetaera* called Archidike 'became a notorious subject of song throughout Greece'.[4]

Accomplished *hetaerae* tended to gravitate towards recognized centres of prostitution, notably ports. Both Rhodopis and Archidike plied their trade in Naucratis, a Greek entrepot on the Nile delta. Another important mecca was Corinth, to which the orator Demosthenes once journeyed to engage the services of a courtesan called Lais. In the event he declined to cough up the princely sum of ten thousand drachmas, which Lais demanded for her services.[5]

Politician's mistress behind Peloponnesian War!

Ironically the most talked-about woman in Athens in the second half of the fifth century BC was probably Pericles' 'common-law wife' Aspasia. Aspasia was able to attain this status because she came from Miletus in Asia Minor and was therefore not subject to the same social constraints as her Athenian counterparts. Her hobnobbing with the leading intellectuals of her day – inconceivable in the case of a freeborn Athenian woman – was sexually transgressive, and it no doubt greatly offended male sensibilities.

Apart from the fact that she had a relationship with Pericles and was accepted into his social circle, we know virtually nothing about Aspasia, though she probably came from a privileged background (her father's name was Axiochus, which means 'Respectable' or 'Respected'). The earliest description of her occurs in Plutarch's biography of Pericles, which was written more than half a millennium after her death. We don't know how old she was when she first met Pericles, nor what the couple saw in each other, nor how long their union lasted. Their domestic circumstances are a complete blank. All we know is that she bore him a son, who was also named Pericles.

Aspasia must have possessed considerable intellectual and social skills to hold her own in a circle which included the philosopher Anaxagoras and the sculptor Pheidias. In Plato's *Menexenus* Socrates credits her with being the true author of Pericles' funeral speech. In the same facetious vein the comic dramatists accused Aspasia of being a kind of latter-day Helen of Troy, whose shenanigans triggered the outbreak of the Peloponnesian War.

Lacking any testimony from Aspasia herself, we've no idea how she may have reacted to this kind of gossip. It's entirely possible that she enjoyed the controversy that she caused. After all, no woman living in Athens had ever enjoyed so much notoriety. When her partner died, their son became naturalized as an Athenian citizen – an exceptional honour for the offspring of a union involving a non-Athenian. Either Aspasia had finally won a place in the hearts of the Athenians or, more plausibly, the state had seen fit to bestow this distinction on its most eminent statesman in spite of the mother's reputation. Thenceforth a veil is drawn over Aspasia in the sources, as typically happens to women whose high visibility derives primarily from their association with a famous man.

Top courtesan topless in court!

The most illustrious courtesan in Athens in the fourth century BC was a Boeotian called Phryne (her name means 'Toad', which is apparently a reference to her swarthy complexion). Like many of her profession, Phryne was born into poverty. Most of the surviving sources for her life are dated long after her death, by which time she had been assigned an emblematic beauty that set her head and shoulders above virtually every other *hetaera*. How much of the biographical tradition is true we shall never know, though it is certain that her celebrity extended far beyond Athens. She seems to have had a talent for titillation. Legend has it that when she appeared 'before the gaze of all the Greeks' at the Eleusinian Mysteries and later at the festival of Poseidon on Aegina, she only removed her outer cloak before stepping into the water to purify herself. She is also said to have been the model both for Praxiteles' nude statue of Aphrodite (see above) and for Apelles' painting of Aphrodite rising from the sea.

Phryne's renown must have peaked when an Athenian named Euthias accused her of having illegally introduced a foreign god into the city – a charge which carried the death penalty. Her defendant was Hyperides, a celebrity of sorts with a reputation for being a ladies' man. When Hyperides realized that the jury was going to find his client guilty, he took the bold step of producing her in court. In Athenaeus' words he then 'tore off Phryne's clothing to expose her breasts and broke into such piteous wailing at the sight of her as he closed his appeal that the jurors, in fear of Aphrodite's humble ministrant, became overcome with compassion and so acquitted her'. The story proved irresistible and it turns up repeatedly over the course of the next five hundred years. Whether it was true or not, this would not have been the first time the Athenians proved susceptible to celebrity's allure (see p. 69 above).[6]

Like other internationally renowned courtesans, Phryne's appetite for fame was prodigious. She offered to finance the rebuilding of the walls of Thebes destroyed by Alexander the Great on condition that they bore an inscription recording her generosity. In so doing, she was following in a long tradition: Rhodopis, whom we mentioned earlier, was the one to begin the trend of conspicuous gift-giving by dedicating some bronze spits at Delphi. Other high-class courtesans made lavish dedicatory offerings and even helped to finance the building of temples. Some were also honoured by ostentious grave monuments, paid for either by themselves or by their grateful clients.

Bride is bridegroom's sister!

One of the most daring attention-seekers in Hellenistic times was the much-married Arsinoë II, a Macedonian princess of exceptional intelligence and natural gifts. Arsinoë's first marriage was to Lysimachus, king of Thrace, who gave her scope to develop her political skills by appointing her ruler of Anatolia (today north-west Turkey), notwithstanding the fact that there were some thirty-five years separating them in age. On Lysimachus' death in 281 BC, Arsinoë briefly married her half-brother Ptolemy Ceraunus ('Thunderbolt'). The union proved less than harmonious. After he had murdered two of her sons, she fled to Egypt, where in the mid-270s she persuaded her full brother Ptolemy II Philadelphus ('Sister-loving', as he came to be called after his death) to divorce his wife and marry her instead.

Though the practice of brother-sister marriage is documented in Egypt in Pharaonic times, we know of no examples among the royal family after the tenth century BC – a gap of over seven hundred years before Arsinoë's appearance on the scene.[7] The marriage would certainly have scandalized Alexandrian Greeks, not to mention the rest of the Greek-speaking world. Brother and sister probably calculated that the support that they would win from native-born Egyptians by reviving an ancient and venerated tradition was worth the price of the obloquy that their action aroused among Greeks. Later Ptolemies regularly adopted the same practice, thereby bestowing upon their queens a prominence that was unique to Egypt.

Some time in the 260s the royal pair were deified as *theoi adelphoi* ('brother-sister gods'). Arsinoë thus became the first western woman to be deified in her lifetime – potent testimony to the force of her personality. She was equated both with Aphrodite Euploia ('Of the prosperous voyage') and with Zephyritis, the personification of the west wind. Far from being aloof and disengaged, she seems to have reached out to the hearts of the common people in a manner that foreshadows Eva Perón. This is indicated by the fact that dedications were made to her as a goddess without official prompting during her lifetime, not only in Egypt but also elsewhere in the eastern Mediterranean.

Single mum rebuffs royal suitor!

Virtually the only way for a respectable Roman *matrona* to achieve renown in the Late Republic was by presenting herself as the epitome of uxorial and maternal self-sacrifice. A shining example was Cornelia, daughter of the famous general Scipio Africanus, who became celebrated for remaining loyal to the memory of her dead husband, even, it was alleged, to the extent of rejecting an offer of marriage from one of the Ptolemies. The suitor in question was probably Ptolemy VIII Euergetes II, nicknamed Physkon or Fatso.[8] Cornelia devoted all her energies to the education of her two sons, Tiberius and Gaius Gracchus, both of whom grew up to become tribunes of the plebs (nine other children died in early childhood). Plutarch, who greatly admired her, reports that after Tiberius and Gaius had both been killed in separate acts of civil violence, Cornelia went to live at Misenum in the bay of Naples. There, far from living a life of retirement, she entertained her guests with stirring accounts of the famous men in her life.

Although Cornelia was highly respected, we can hardly suppose that she attracted a popular following, far less that she became a celebrity. Her elevation to quasi-mythical status as a pillar of virtue no doubt occurred mainly after her death, even though she probably began cultivating this image during her lifetime. Consistent with the position of women in Roman society, Cornelia was able to achieve renown precisely because she was a widow and therefore under no obligation to subordinate her personality to that of her husband. Even so, it is important to note that her primary claim to fame was as 'the daughter of Africanus and mother of the Gracchi', as the inscription on the pedestal of her statue makes clear.

There is nothing in the record to suggest that Cornelia was regarded as particularly interesting in her own right, though she was credited with being extremely learned. We might even go so far as to say that her prominence was the consequence of her unqualified acquiescence in the gender-stereotyping of her day. Other Republican *matronae* who won distinction for acts of self-sacrifice include Sulpicia, who was judged by her peers to be 'the most chaste' and given the honour of dedicating a statue of Venus Verticordia ('True-hearted') to raise the standard of female morality in Rome,[9] and Turia, who heroically saved her husband's life when he was proscribed by Octavian and Mark Antony in *c.* 43 BC.[10]

Even the wives of the most influential politicians were largely invisible, due in part to the discrepancy in years between them and their husbands. Calpurnia, for instance, was barely sixteen when she married the forty-something Julius Caesar. She enters the historical record only on the morning of her husband's murder for failing to dissuade him from attending the Senate. After that she disappears without trace. As his wife, she probably lived a life of virtual seclusion, like every other well-bred and well-behaved married woman of her day. Indeed she may have been under a special compulsion to do so in view of the fact that Caesar had divorced his previous wife Pompeia on account of suspicions of sexual misconduct.

Even Augustus' wife Livia was not particularly prominent in the lifetime of her husband.[11] Though undoubtedly more powerful than any Roman woman had been before her, she operated entirely behind the scenes. And even when she was adopted into the imperial family on Augustus' death as Iulia Augusta in AD 14, her son Tiberius, who largely owed his position as emperor to her ruthless intriguing, blocked efforts to provide her with an officially sanctioned role in the state. Immediately after her husband's death, however, Tiberius did authorize the minting of a coin series with Augustus' head on the obverse and Livia's on the reverse, bearing the inscription *Iulia Augusta Genetrix Orbis* ('Mother of the World') – a title that is not associated with any other Roman empress. Even so, it was only as the promoter of the cult of the deified Augustus that she attained a public position of sorts – by presenting herself, in other words, in the traditional role of a dutiful widow, whose mission in life was to burnish the First Citizen's memory.

Roman aristocrat in bed with red!

To make the headlines in Republican Rome a girl had to throw modesty to the winds and indulge in outrageously risqué behaviour. This is exactly what Sempronia, a consul's daughter, is alleged to have done. The historian Sallust classifies her among a number of women (he mentions no others by name) who in their youth made fortunes as prostitutes. When their looks faded, they fell on hard times and used their connections to serve the interests of a dangerous revolutionary named Lucius Sergius Catilina, who, following his unsuccessful bid for the consulship in 63 and again in 62 BC, fomented social unrest.

In Sallust's opinion, Sempronia had all the qualities that would have made her a hot news item today. She was attractive, well-educated, witty, and endowed with a voracious sexual appetite. In fact, 'she was so consumed with lust that she more often made advances to men than they did to her'.[12] Much of the scorn that he heaps upon her, in particular the charge that she committed 'acts of masculine daring', is due to the fact that she rejected the conventional stereotype of the Roman *matrona*. Yet even Sallust cannot refrain from paying tribute to Sempronia's intellectual qualities, by noting that she wrote poetry and was an excellent conversationalist.

Imperial nympho holds sexual stamina record!

With the accession of the Julio-Claudians, women of the imperial household began defying convention in ways that had been previously unimaginable. They did so perhaps primarily to advance their political ambitions. They seem, moreover, to have done little to conceal these ambitions, notwithstanding the huge risks they were taking.

The first to break with the traditional mould was the Elder Agrippina, the wife of Germanicus and Augustus' grand-daughter. Agrippina was such a forceful personality that she became the founder of a populist political faction. When, moreover, the legions on the Rhine were threatening to mutiny, it was she who stepped in to quell the unrest. Agrippina accompanied her husband in his ill-judged tour of Egypt in AD 19, which, as we saw earlier (p. 62), drew ecstatic responses from the local population. They may well have been the first celebrity husband and wife team in history. After Germanicus' death in the East, she returned to Italy with his ashes. She was greeted by grief-stricken crowds lining the route from Brundisium to Rome, hailing her 'the glory of her country', 'the sole offspring of Augustus', and 'the epitome of traditional virtue'[13].

Once back in the capital, Agrippina continued to grab the headlines, this time by playing the role of the devoted Roman widow. Her popularity with the army and the populace aroused the suspicions of the Emperor Tiberius, which were intensified by her outspoken hints that he had been involved in her husband's death. When she publicly refused food at a banquet in the imperial palace for fear that it was poisoned, she deliberately created a scandal. In AD 29 Tiberius banished her to Pandateria, a remote islet due west of Naples, where she eventually starved herself to death.

The Emperor Claudius' third wife Messalina was also a headline-grabber, albeit in a rather different mould.[14] On the basis of Tacitus' portrait of her, she has been described as 'one of the great nympho-maniacs of history'. Messalina allegedly ran a brothel in the imperial palace, employing women of aristocratic status as prostitutes and using their husbands as pimps. She also held the record for having sex with the most number of partners over a twenty-four hour period, thereby beating the record of the reigning champion – a notorious prostitute.[15] (Messalina's score was twenty-five!) Anecdotes of this sort no doubt reflect the scandalous talk about her on the streets of Rome during her lifetime.

Even though the lurid details of Messalina's sex life have all but obscured her political talents, it is evident that she was instrumental in repelling several threats to her husband's life and position during their eight years of marriage.[14] Her end came when she consummated in public a mock-marriage with the consul-designate for AD 48. As soon as Claudius found out, he ordered her execution. True to form, she forestalled the soldiers who were sent to arrest her by taking her own life.

Egyptian scientists discover woman with brain!

Outside royal and imperial circles there were very few outlets for women with brains. It says much about the hostility which women physicians faced that in order to achieve professional recognition a certain Agnodice is said to have disguised herself as a man. There were several first-rate Greek poetesses, including Sappho of Lesbos, Corinna of Tanagra, Erinna of Telos, and Anyte of Tegea, and at least one mural painter, Helena of Alexandria, but we know very little about their lives. The only Roman poetess whom we know of is Sulpicia, a contemporary of Horace and Vergil. The fact that her poems were wrongly attributed to the elegiac poet Tibullus suggests, however, that her profile was extremely low. She is, moreover, the only woman who made it into the corpus of surviving classical Latin literature. There was also a handful of female scholars and philosophers, though none of them belonged to the first rank.

Virtually the only female celebrity intellectual of late antiquity was Hypatia of Alexandria (*c.* 370-415). Hypatia was quite possibly the leading mathematician of her day, though no original works of hers have survived. Her celebrity, however, seems to have derived mainly from the fact that she achieved mastery of a traditionally male discipline. The contemporary church historian Socrates Scholasticus writes: 'Hypatia reached such heights of wisdom that she far surpassed all the philosophers in her circle .... She expounded all the [Neoplatonist] doctrines in her addresses to a free public... and people would come from everywhere to engage in philosophy with her.'[16] Not surprisingly, she was also credited with great beauty. The entry under her name in the *Suda*, a tenth-century Byzantine lexicon, claims that her students routinely fell in love with her. It also states that she wore the traditional cape of a Cynic philosopher and 'went about the city freely, expounding the philosophy of Plato, Aristotle and other philosophers to anyone who felt like listening to her'.

To practise mathematics Hypatia would certainly have had to engage in open debate with men, and this in itself would have made her an object of considerable interest to the Alexandrians. She raised her profile yet further by dabbling in politics. In particular she became a spokesperson in negotiations between the Alexandrian church and Orestes, the Roman-appointed prefect of Egypt. Though this initially won her considerable influence, when relations between Orestes and Cyril, the archbishop, broke down, Hypatia became a scapegoat and was accused of being a pagan sympathizer. She was stripped naked and dragged to the cathedral, where she was cut to pieces with oyster shells at the hands of a rabble of self-professed Christians.

Afterlife

Phryne remained a vibrant figure in literary discourse until the fifth century AD. To lie in bed beside her without making any sexual advances was the mark of a true philosopher.[17] She was one among a select group of *hetaerae* whose physical attractions and witticisms (many of them obscene) form the subject of Book 13 of Athenaeus' *Sophists at Dinner*, which serves as a tribute to the profession in general. In light of the work's dramatic context, we might dismiss the comments made at the table as typical of the kind of scurrilous gossip that circulates in an all-male gathering when drink flows freely. Far from this being idle tittle-tattle, however, Athenaeus culls his information from a wide range of lost treatises, which demonstrates that *hetaerae* had a secure place in the informal historical record. Phryne dedicated a gilt statue of herself by Praxiteles at Delphi, flanked on either side by statues of Apollo. Though this was described by the Cynic philosopher Crates as 'a monument to Greek incontinence', we need hardly doubt that her fellow Thespians would have taken considerable pride in their compatriot.[18] The story of her trial became a set piece in the work of rhetoricians, who regularly cited Euthias' baring of her breasts as an unconventional but highly successful instance of the appeal to pity.

Arsinoë's posthumous fame did much to advance the dynastic ambitions of the Ptolemaic royal house. After her death in 268 BC gold and silver coins were minted in her honour, depicting her wearing the horns of the god Ammon. A region of Egypt known as the Fayum was re-named Arsinoïtes. A cult of Arsinoë Philadelphos, which was administered by a dedicated priestess, is already attested for the year after her death. Egyptian games known as the Arsinoeia were established in her honour. Numerous Aegean ports were also named after her.

The image of Cornelia as the quintessentially devoted Roman

mother who bore the tragic loss of her sons with exemplary fortitude endured into the Imperial era.[19] The statue that was set up in her honour in Rome probably in Republican times was known to Pliny the Elder.[20] St Jerome claims that her wisdom was such that the philosopher Carneades conversed with her.[21]

Though the Senate voted divine honours to Livia on her death, Tiberius vetoed the move, claiming, somewhat improbably, that she would not have wanted them. Livia was finally deified by her grandson Claudius, primarily, one suspects, so that the emperor could claim the title 'grandson of a goddess'. After Claudius' death, her cult disappears and there are very few references to her in later literature.

Messalina forms the climax to Juvenal's catalogue of unchaste women in *Satire* VI, where she is described as performing the services of a prostitute in a seedy brothel in a vain attempt to satisfy her insatiable lust.[22]

Hypatia's posthumous reputation probably owed less to her mathematical skills than to the violent and horrific circumstances of her highly controversial death. John, Bishop of Nikiû,[23] who flourished in the latter part of the seventh century, presents the lynching as a justifiable action taken by a flock of believers, whereas Socrates Scholasticus represented it as a terrible act of infamy.

The Tabloid Queen

Being a princess isn't all it's cracked up to be.
Diana, Princess of Wales

The women whose lives we investigated in the previous chapter won celebrity either as a result of their willingness to flout convention or because of their attachment to a powerful male. Few of them, however, were able to use their celebrity to consolidate a position of long-lasting political influence. Among all the women in history who have established themselves as leading players on the world stage, two of the most spectacular and accomplished are Cleopatra Queen of Egypt and the Byzantine Empress Theodora. Had they been alive today, they would certainly have been the constant targets of scandal hunters. Even in the absence of the paparazzi, however, Cleopatra and Theodora were still the object of endless gossip. They are also practically the only women from classical antiquity whose lives are known to us in sufficient detail to make them the subject of modern full-length biographies. Theodora, who came from the bottom of the social heap, was able to reinvent herself by becoming the emperor's ideal wife. No such option was available to Cleopatra, whose image as a foreign sorceress and seductress remains to this day the product of Octavian's highly effective propaganda machine.

Foreign queen in illicit love nest!

It was Cleopatra VII Thea Philopator ('Goddess and Lover of the Father [or Fatherland]'), destined to be the last reigning Ptolemaic monarch, who came closest to achieving the kind of star status that we today associate with a Liz Taylor or a Julia Roberts. The name Cleopatra, which contains the word *kleos*, 'glory', actually means either 'glorifying the father' or 'the glory of her father'. Though in the final years of her life Cleopatra's renown was almost wholly obscured by the contempt she acquired as a result of her liaison with Mark Antony, her consummate show-womanship enabled her to achieve an unprecedented level of political influence in the Roman world.

Cleopatra became joint ruler of Egypt with her younger brother and husband Ptolemy XIII at the age of eighteen. Though her mother's identity is uncertain, she was almost certainly a Greek, because the Ptolemies, as we noted earlier, adopted the Egyptian practice of brother-sister marriage. In the Roman tradition, however, she is consistently depicted as a native, dark-skinned Egyptian. Whether, like Liz Taylor, who took her part in Joseph L. Mankiewicz's blockbuster *Cleopatra* (1963), Cleopatra was drop-dead gorgeous seems doubtful, at least if her coin portraits are anything to go by.[1] The ones which date to the latter half of her twenty-one year reign depict a somewhat unprepossessing woman with a hooked nose, jutting chin, rolls of neck fat and deep-set eyes. No sex goddess then, or at least not a numismatic one. Several three-dimensional portraits of attractive women in what is sometimes referred to as 'a style resembling Cleopatra' have also been identified, but there is no consensus as to which (if any) depict the 'real' Cleopatra.[2]

Very possibly Cleopatra's charms were more intellectual than physical, which indeed is what Plutarch suggests. He writes: 'Her beauty, we're told, wasn't incomparable and it didn't completely knock you off your feet. But conversing with her was quite something, and the charm of her presence ... was irresistible.'[3] Though it may seem somewhat surprising from a modern perspective that Cleopatra did not choose to be depicted in a more flattering light, possibly she calculated that if she presented herself as an object of delectation for the male gaze, she would have compromised her political authority.

Cleopatra first drew the attention of the Roman world by embarking on a highly publicized sexual relationship with Julius Caesar when the latter arrived in Alexandria in 48 BC after defeating Pompey in the Civil War. Whether or not she was delivered to him wrapped up in a carpet as legend has it is of little historical significance, although this fanciful anecdote does appositely convey the image of a woman who was prepared to employ highly unconventional methods to achieve her political goals. Following the death of Ptolemy XIII and Caesar's departure from Egypt, Cleopatra openly proclaimed her liai-

132

son with the Dictator by naming her newborn son Ptolemy Caesar. He acquired the nickname Caesarion or 'Little Caesar'. Numerous inscriptions and images were dedicated to Caesarion, though most of them were later destroyed by Octavian. One of the most impressive surviving examples is a massive bas-relief depicting Cleopatra and Caesarion, aged between eight to eleven, making offerings to the gods, which was carved into the south wall of the Temple of Hathor at Dendera in Upper Egypt.

Whether Caesar was actually the father, indeed whether Cleopatra actually believed him to be the father, is another matter altogether. The queen might well have calculated that she had everything to gain by boasting of their affair since it would have increased her standing on the world stage. It made her more visible – and therefore more powerful. How Caesar himself responded to the boast – or how for that matter his long-suffering wife Calpurnia bore it – is also not recorded, though the fact that his agent, a knight named Caius Oppius, circulated a pamphlet seeking to disprove his paternity strongly suggests that he was sufficiently irked to initiate a policy of damage control. It would be fascinating to know just how Oppius sought to exculpate the Dictator. Taxing Cleopatra with another sexual liaison was presumably not an option, since that would have had consequences for Caesar's reputation for *machismo*.

In 46 BC Cleopatra and her new brother-husband Ptolemy XIV arrived in Rome as Caesar's official guests. They remained there for well over a year and were still in residence at the time of his assassination in 44 BC. Though there is no report of any private contact between Caesar and Cleopatra during this period, it is highly likely that they resumed their affair, particularly in light of the fact that Caesar placed his luxury villa on the Janiculan Hill overlooking the Tiber at the couple's disposal. A gilded statue of the queen was erected in the new Temple of Venus Genetrix in the Julian Forum, thereby giving her almost equal status with Venus herself. The rumour-mongers and graffiti-writers surely had a field day.

From kiss to this!

Lacking as we do any Egyptian testimony, we see Cleopatra almost wholly through the eyes of her Roman detractors. But how did her subjects perceive her? Did they regard her as a dizzy airhead, who brought disgrace to the throne of Egypt? Or as a dedicated patriot, who preserved her country's semi-independence far longer than might have been expected? Certainly Egypt, though essentially powerless in this period, was seeking to regain its former prestige on the world stage. How her subjects later responded to Octavian's slandering of her, assuming that it penetrated their consciousness, is also a mystery to us.

A consummate self-promoter, Cleopatra mounted some of the most thrilling pageants ever staged. She is alleged to have taken a spectacular voyage up the Nile with Caesar. Though some historians have argued that the river trip was the figment of later imagination, the staging of such a high profile event certainly fits with Cleopatra's political ambitions, even if the report of it grew out of all proportion. The sight of their queen beside the most powerful man in the Roman world would have sent a strong signal of her political importance to her people, particularly since the luxuriating pair were accompanied by a sizeable contingent of Caesar's troops. Cleopatra's arrival in Rome is also likely to have been carefully stage-managed, though no record of it has survived.

Her most brilliantly conceived 'photo-op' took place in 41 BC at Tarsus in Cilicia (southern Turkey) in the presence of Mark Antony. Antony had summoned the queen to account for her lukewarm behaviour during the recent war against Caesar's assassins. Eschewing the role of petitioner, Cleopatra completely upstaged Antony by mobilizing all the pomp and ceremony of her Egyptian court. Plutarch's description of their meeting on the banks of the River Cydnus, which provided the inspiration for the famous passage in Shakespeare's *Antony and Cleopatra*, reads as follows:

> She had such scornful contempt for Antony that she sailed up the river in a barge with a gilded poop, its purple sails spread out, its rowers moving it forward with silver oars to the tune of the flute, in harmony with pipes and lyres. She herself reclined beneath a gold-spangled awning, decked out to resemble Aphrodite, while boys resembling painted cupids stood on either side of her. Likewise the most beautiful of her female attendants, dressed up like Nymphs and Graces, stood at the rudders and at the ropes.

Wonderful scents discharged by numerous incense-burners drifted across the banks of the river. Some people accompanied her upstream from the mouth of the river, while others went down from the city to gaze upon her. When the entire crowd in the market place had gone to behold her, Antony was left sitting by himself on his platform. The report circulated that Aphrodite was revelling with Dionysus for the benefit of Asia.[4]

This was grand-standing on an epic scale. But it was not mere posturing for posturing's sake. On the contrary, it had a profound political import. Within the space of five years Cleopatra had acquired control of parts of Cilicia, parts of Judaea, Cyprus, Phoenicia and Arabia. In 34 BC her manoeuvrings culminated in a magnificent ceremony known as the 'Donations of Alexandria', ostensibly held in celebration of Antony's victory over the king of Armenia, at which the foundation of a great oriental kingdom was announced. Mark Antony accorded her and Caesarion the titles 'Queen of Kings' and 'King of Kings' respectively. In addition, he assigned portions of the Eastern Empire to his and Cleopatra's six-year-old twins, who had been named, somewhat preposterously, Alexander Helios (Sun) and Cleopatra Selene (Moon). The event was celebrated with the minting of silver *denarii* bearing the presumptuous legend 'Queen of kings and of children who are kings'.

Asp slays queen!

Precisely how Octavian went about the task of besmirching Cleopatra's reputation in preparation for his eventual showdown with Antony is not known, though all he actually needed to do was mobilize that age-old weapon, rumour. He was after all the master of spin. Indeed he might almost be claimed as its inventor.

Octavian and his agents cast Cleopatra in the role of an archetypal barbarian witch and seductress. His success with this strategy is all the more striking in view of the fact that Cleopatra is credited with only two long-standing extra-marital affairs. In fact for over half her adult life she may well have been sexually abstemious. Vilified as a native Egyptian with an insatiable sexual appetite, she now became every upstanding Roman's worst nightmare – or, if not his nightmare, certainly the antithesis of the ideal Roman wife, who embodied *pudici-tia* or chastity. Antony was cast in the role of an ageing gigolo who had abandoned his duty to become a mere 'prosthetic' of the queen, in Plutarch's haunting phrase.[5] When hostilities broke out, Octavian ostentatiously declared war on Cleopatra alone, evidently to signal that his Roman enemy was beneath contempt.

To this day, it is impossible to establish the dividing line between the truth and the lies. It has recently been suggested that the report of Cleopatra's death by the poisonous fangs of an asp, which is first recorded by Plutarch a century and a quarter after the event, was a fabrication on Octavian's part. Certainly the circumstances surrounding her death, to the extent that they can be reconstructed, lend some support to this theory. It was, after all, Octavian's men who 'discovered' her body, so if he did give orders for her to be murdered, the crime would never have come to light anyway. It was, moreover, in Octavian's long-term interests to have Cleopatra removed, even though there was short-term political cost in circulating the story of her suicide, since this aroused the sympathies of some Romans, Horace among them, as well as those of her subjects.[6]

Working-class girl nabs heir to throne!

Theodora (*c*. 497-548), who rose from the gutter to become the wife and trusted confidante of the Emperor Justinian, was one of the most accomplished social climbers of all time. The only woman who comes close to her in late antiquity is Helena, the wife (or concubine) of Constantius I and the mother of Constantine the Great, who rose from the position of innkeeper to become dowager empress with the title Augusta in AD 324.

As the daughter of a bear-feeder who worked in the Hippodrome in Constantinople, Theodora could hardly have come from more inauspicious beginnings. As a one-time mime who performed sex acts on stage, she could not have faced greater obstacles in her path towards the imperial purple. She was only sixteen when she first met Justinian; he was more than twice her age. Her marriage was the most scandalous that the Empire had ever known. In order to wed her, Justinian had to persuade his uncle, the Emperor Justin, to abolish the law which prohibited a senator from marrying a former prostitute and to elevate Theodora to the rank of a patrician. Her meteoric rise naturally aroused deep resentment among the upper echelons of society, since she exemplified the greatest possible threat to the stability of the social order.

Theodora has left no personal testimony behind her, and it is greatly to her disadvantage that the most important source for her life is the so-called *Secret History* by Procopius of Caesarea, in which she is depicted as a sadistic vamp and arch-manipulator. A lawyer and rhetorician by profession, Procopius served as legal advisor and private secretary to Justinian's great general Belisarius. The *Secret History*, which *Newsweek Magazine* recently described as 'one of the supreme hatchet jobs of all time', savages not only the reputation of Theodora herself, but also those of Justinian, Belisarius and Belisarius' wife Antonia. Procopius also wrote official accounts of Justinian's reign called *Wars* and *Buildings*, which depict both emperor and empress in a very different light.

Procopius does not tell us how Theodora managed to attract the eye of the man who would become renowned for assembling into a single work the legal opinions of all the leading Roman jurists – one of the greatest legacies of antiquity. Very likely Justinian regularly consorted with members of the demi-monde, like so many potentates and royals both before and since. According to Procopius, 'She was neither a pipe-player nor a harpist, nor did she have any expertise in dancing, but she sold her beauty to all and sundry, plying her trade with almost every inch of her body.'[7] Her sex appeal may have been what initially drew Justinian to her, but by itself it can hardly have kept him faithful all those years. The only explanation Procopius gives for the influence that she achieved in an essentially male-dominated and militaristic society is her unrivalled talent for intrigue and her mastery of the black arts. The truth, however, is that Theodora must have been extremely intelligent, though whether she was educated is something of a mystery. We don't even know for certain whether she was literate, though in view of the fact that she could hold her own in the most educated circle in the land it would be surprising indeed if she wasn't.

Procopius' vitriolic attack on Theodora takes the form of a pious homily on the lasciviousness of women in general and of female performers in particular. He famously reports that it was her custom to lie naked on the floor of the theatre while specially trained geese picked at grains of barley that had been sprinkled over her private parts.[8] One can almost see the old prude salaciously licking his lips as he writes. Her cruelty, he alleges, was as unbridled as her lust: so far did she lack even the vestiges of a maternal instinct that she not only procured several abortions, but also contrived the murder of her only son.

Yet of all the celebrities from antiquity of whom we have record none more dramatically re-invented herself than this actress turned empress – an accomplishment for which Procopius fails to give her any credit. For after she married Justinian, Theodora set out to fashion herself into a model of wifely devotion, a role which she played to consummate perfection throughout their twenty-three years of wedlock. Even Procopius can tax her with only a single indiscretion, and this is suspect, being otherwise unattested.

Theodora also used her theatrical talents to bolster her husband's flagging spirits at the supreme crisis of his career, and in so doing may have changed the course of history. The year 532 saw one of the worst episodes of civil violence in Roman history – the so-called Nika Riot, named from '*Nika*!', 'Victory!', the rallying cry of the Blues and Greens, rival supporters of the chariot teams which competed in the races in the Hippodrome, which now united in an uprising against the emperor. Half of Constantinople perished in the ensuing conflagration and some thirty thousand insurgents were put to the sword. Theodora, as Procopius relates in the *Wars*, signalled her determination not to yield to the temptation of flight by defiantly declaring in the Senate, 'I hope I am never separated from the imperial purple nor live to see the day when the people I meet fail to address me as empress .... I approve the old saying that kingship makes a glorious winding sheet.'[9] Rousing words indeed. Justinian took them to heart and stood his ground. The riot was quelled, though whether the empress won any plaudits from her subjects goes unrecorded.

The tabloids would certainly have had a field day with Theodora's life-story today, not least because of its sensational 'from rags to riches' angle. Instead of the tabloids, however, there was only crusty old Procopius, who wisely refrained from publishing his history during his subject's lifetime, as the original title of his work, *Anecdota* or 'Things not intended for circulation', indicates. Magazines such as *Now*, *OK!* and *Glamour* were still light years away.

Though Procopius' portrait of Theodora is a self-conscious literary creation, the venom he heaped upon her was probably not unrepresentative of the majority of his upper-class readers, consistent as it was with the widespread distrust of female sexuality that was endemic throughout antiquity. The image of the ambitious upstart who dominated her weak and vacillating husband through intrigue and sex would surely have proved irresistible, and though there is no particular reason to suppose that Procopius was its inventor, he was in an excellent position to add fuel to the flames.

It certainly didn't help matters that Theodora's husband was himself a parvenu of peasant extraction, whose elevation was due to the unexpected accession of his uncle Justin. The fact that she was of lowly birth, the fact that she rose to a position of unprecedented authority, and the fact that she claimed equality with the emperor – all this was more than enough to make her reviled in the eyes of those who feared that with two upstarts on the throne, the world was turning topsy-turvy. The fact that she was so much more than just the sum of these parts surely made her the most talked about woman of late antiquity. Even so, not everyone would have regarded her as a manipulative bimbo. On the contrary, she may have served as a fantasy role model for women of humble origin, by holding out the fairytale possibility of social elevation through marriage.

The famous mosaic in the chancel of San Vitale in Ravenna, which was dedicated a year before Theodora's death possibly from cancer at about the age of fifty, provides a very different image from that of the *Secret History*. The empress is distinguished from her companions both by her size and by the nimbus, symbolic of her divinely sanctioned status, that surrounds her head. She wears an elaborate pearl diadem that encircles her hair and almost overshadows her face. Long strings of pearls hang down from the diadem on either side. A ceremonial collar, also made of pearls, rests on her shoulders. Gold earrings, in the shape of hoops weighted with pendant jewels, adorn her ears. A purple cloak with gold embroidered borders reaches all the way down to her bejewelled and gold-trimmed shoes. Endlessly reproduced in modern times, the Ravenna mosaic has set the seal on Theodora's physical appearance for all time as a statuesque, aloof and mysterious beauty.[10] We do not know whether she connived in creating this image.

Since, however, it is consistent with the exalted status that she claimed for herself at court, it is entirely likely that she did.

The Ravenna mosaic is the only positively identified extant portrait of Theodora, though we have literary allusions to several statues that are now lost, including one that stood on top of a porphyry column in the capital.[11] A mosaic of Justinian and Theodora, celebrating their victories over the Vandals and the Goths, decorated the vestibule of the imperial palace in Constantinople. Even so, Theodora's face would not have been particularly well-known. Like all empresses, she was heavily veiled whenever she travelled in her litter, which meant that her subjects would rarely have caught a glimpse of her. Yet by the end of her life she had become a secular saint: no mean achievement for a humble bear-keeper's daughter.

Afterlife

Cleopatra's reputation has proved far more durable than that of any other woman from classical antiquity, due principally to the fact that she had affairs with two of the most powerful men of her day and made an audacious bid for a measure of control over the Roman Empire. Since her subjects have left nothing to help us to flesh out her portrait, she remains to this day largely the product of Roman propaganda.

Her story provided fodder for the Augustan poets, who for the most part acquiesced in the stereotypical image that the emperor fabricated. Propertius places her at the climax to his catalogue of controlling women as 'one who was screwed by her slaves' and as 'the harlot queen of foul Canopus'.[12] In a famous ode written shortly after her death, Horace purports to convey the mood of jubilation to which the announcement gave rise. 'Now is the time for drinking and beating the ground with wild abandon,' he declares at the beginning of the poem. He ends, however, on a much more sober note, describing her suicide as an act of courage that spared her the indignity of being conveyed to Rome and displayed in a triumph.[13] Vergil's characterization of Dido, whose steamy affair with Aeneas keeps the gossip mills in Carthage grinding away, undoubtedly prompted comparison with the Egyptian queen, since her attempt to seduce Aeneas into abandoning his mission to found the Roman race mirrors in the hostile propaganda the depiction of Cleopatra's seduction of Mark Antony. Even so, Vergil's Dido is by no means unsympathetically portrayed.

Cleopatra is favourably mentioned by the Alexandrian grammarian Apion in the 30s AD. The fourth-century AD historian Ammianus Marcellinus complains that the Egyptians were still venerating her memory in his day.[17] She also seems to have served as a kind of posthumous pin-up. A terracotta relief depicting a Nilotic scene shows a man and a woman, possibly intended to represent Antony and herself, copulating doggy-style. Even more salacious is the portrayal on a Roman lamp of a naked woman, thought to be Cleopatra, being impregnated by a generously endowed crocodile.[14]

Although Octavian destroyed all the portrait statues which Antony had erected of himself in Alexandria, he left those of Cleopatra standing. He did so allegedly because one of her supporters gave him two thousand talents to save them from destruction. He may also have calculated that this gesture of political reconciliation would help to mollify her grieving subjects.[15] The statue which Julius Caesar erected to Cleopatra in the Temple of Venus Genetrix in the Julian Forum was still standing in the third century AD, so that the queen 'though defeated and captured, was in fact glorified', as the historian Dio shrewdly observed.[16] The so-called 'Cleopatreion' temple in Rosetta (modern Rashid) may have been dedicated to her worship. A graffito from the island of Philae in Upper Egypt dated to the fourth century AD testifies to the esteem of her fellow-Egyptians. Early Islamic culture venerated her as a saviour.[17]

Theodora's posthumous appeal was greatly enhanced by the fact that she left behind an utterly devoted husband. Justinian named several foundations after her, the most notable of which was the town of Theodoropolis in Thrace.[18]

Conclusions

You know you don't have no fun at all if you get too famous.
                        Louis Armstrong, jazz musician

I won't be happy until I'm as famous as God.
                        Madonna, entertainer

In the Graeco-Roman world the attainment of celebrity was for the most part a laborious and time-consuming activity. This was because the commodity was in short supply and the means of promoting it extremely limited. It was primarily restricted either to emperors, kings and aristocrats, or to outstandingly gifted individuals whose devotion to their talent raised them above the common mass of humankind. So it tended to be either the reward for a lifetime of exceptional achievement or the consequence of birth. And once earned it tended to stick. There was nothing remotely equivalent to Warhol's fifteen minutes of fame.

In the absence of organized networks of news gathering and news distribution, not to mention today's ever-attentive paparazzi, word of mouth was the primary vehicle for building a reputation, though other methods of self-promotion were employed by those with political and economic clout. These included commissioning encomiastic literature, disseminating portraiture, hosting lavish entertainments, financing public monuments, engaging in creative self-mythologizing, and staging the ancient equivalent of the 'photo-op'. The Hellenistic kings were the first to exploit this to the full, mounting well-attended pageants to promote their shaky dynastic claims.

Politically prominent individuals sometimes sought to ally themselves with well-known personalities either to enhance or to soften their reputations. A notable example is Archelaus, the late fifth-century BC king of Macedon, who played host to the tragic poets Euripides and Agathon, the epic poet Choerilus of Samos, the lyre-player Timotheus of Miletus, and the painter Zeuxis of Heraclea. Others, such as Alexander the Great and Augustus, co-opted the services of men of letters in the hope of securing their endorsement of their political agendas.

There was nothing comparable to the modern press, though it's just possible that Rome's daily gazette, the *acta diurna*, which primarily related official events, occasionally included more sensational news items. In addition, the distribution of leaflets and the painting of graffiti assisted candidates in political elections. As today, graffiti served the unofficial function of announcing to all and sundry simply that '*Decius fuit hic*'.[1]

A handful of enterprising individuals took the pioneering step of promulgating their memoirs, among them Julius Caesar, the Emperor Augustus and St Augustine. Though it wasn't customary to publish biographies of famous people while they were still alive, posthumous biographies, often organized into a collection, such as Diogenes Laertius' *Lives of the Philosophers*, preserved anecdotal data that probably circulated during the subjects' lifetimes.

How many famous individuals became addicted to celebrity is impossible to estimate. Certainly Alcibiades sought the limelight primarily for its own sake, but most politicians did so in pursuit of a particular goal. This was true even of the Emperor Nero, who craved the celebrity of an Olympic crown to gain the goodwill of his subjects, though in his case narcissism also played a significant part.

As the visible and outward expression of the pursuit of honour, celebrity was predominantly the prerogative of élite males. The chapter in Valerius Maximus' *Memorable Deeds and Sayings* entitled 'Those of humble birth who became illustrious' provides only five examples from Roman history and three from Greek.[2] This argues a mindset that assumed that being in the public eye was the prerogative of those of aristocratic birth.

The heyday of the Greek athlete lasted from the final decades of the sixth century BC to the first half of the fifth. Omitting aristocrats who won prizes in equestrian events in which they did not compete and who then did everything to hype their success, the biggest sports stars in the Greek world were those who won prizes for extraordinary feats of strength, whereas in the Roman world charioteers alone became megastars.

Conclusions

Actors achieved their greatest glory in the Hellenistic era in Greece, and in the Late Republican era in Rome. Probably the biggest showbiz celebrities enjoyed a following that was almost equal to that of a modern pop star. In the Imperial era mime and pantomime artists dominated the public stage. Philosophers and poets were celebrities throughout antiquity, as too were physicians. In fact some of the most accomplished Hellenistic portraits are of philosophers and poets. Religious charismatics were also a prominent feature of the celebrity landscape, though they attracted little literary attention and were not commemorated in art.

Though many celebrities had their circles of adoring fans, there is only limited evidence for the all-too-common contemporary phenomenon of 'celebrity worship syndrome' – a pathological fixation upon the lives and personalities of celebrities. No names of any serial killers or mass murderers have come to us, excluding of course Roman Emperors such as Caligula, Nero and Domitian.

For the most part women achieved visibility only if they were prepared to step outside their socially sanctioned roles as wives and mothers. One of the few opportunities for them to enjoy autonomy and solvency, as well as celebrity, was as high-class prostitutes. Female intellectuals were extremely rare. A handful of aristocratic Roman women became idealized as dedicated wives and mothers, but notoriety was the best that most of them could hope to achieve. Those with the highest profile were thought to owe their prominence to the fact that they exploited their sexual charms, notable examples being Aspasia in the Greek world, Sempronia in the Roman world, and Theodora in the Christian world.

Neither Greece nor Rome produced anything resembling a celebrity class similar to the one that evolved in Britain in the 1960s. To what extent ancient celebrities acknowledged a common identity is impossible to determine, though the phenomenon of the 'celebrity wedding' was not unknown, as we see from Democedes' engagement to Milo's daughter.

Though dictators occasionally fraternized with actors, and though emperors occasionally fell madly in love with actresses, such occurrences never posed a serious threat to the stability of the social hierarchy, as did the rise of Twiggy and the Rolling Stones to the

British establishment in the 60s (even though some of the Stones came from a solidly middle-class background).

Apart from members of either an imperial or royal family, virtually no one achieved celebrity status before attaining full adulthood. With the exception of gladiators, a few outstandingly handsome men such as Alcibiades and Antinoüs, Hadrian's constant companion for nine years, and of course prostitutes of international renown, celebrities did not market themselves as objects of erotic fantasy. There is little therefore to suggest that their personalities and bodies were invested with the kind of fantasies and longing that accompany their modern counterparts. If actors, mimes and musicians traded on their looks, we hear nothing about it.

Fame in antiquity was a function of geo-political realities. In the age of the city-state, few individuals had reputations that extended beyond the borders of their own community. The chief exceptions were leading aristocrats and tyrants, whose names sometimes circulated throughout the Greek-speaking world. In the Hellenistic era the opportunities for attention-seeking greatly expanded, due both to the universalizing effect of Alexander's conquests and to the growth in the number and size of public arenas.

An important factor in Roman times was the increase in urbanization, which appreciably enhanced the public's awareness of celebrities. Under the emperors Rome exercised a powerful attraction upon those who were eager to make a particularly big splash. It was, to use a modern phrase, the happening place. Precisely because it offered such rich opportunities for celebrity, Rome came to represent the antithesis of the heavenly city of God from a Christian perspective.

Few celebrities became household faces in antiquity, apart from the politicians and monarchs whose portraits appeared on coins, and even these could hardly hope to achieve the effect of the repeated impact of a face upon the brain that is so readily available today through incessant media attention. Though travel helped to heighten a celebrity's profile, there were some striking anomalies, the most notable being the pillar saints, whose celebrity was a precise function of their immobility. The lives of recluses sometimes attracted considerable attention as well, as we see from the career of Diogenes the Cynic.

Modern society indiscriminately showers celebrity status on footballers, media tarts, rock stars and popes, making their contributions to society virtually indistinguishable. Both in Britain and in the USA reality television game shows such as 'I'm a Celebrity: Get Me Out Of Here' and 'I Want A Famous Face' pander to our seemingly endless fascination with what it means to be famous, rather than with what it takes, or what it should take, to achieve fame. It is a fascination that speaks to a sterile narcissism that now courses irresistibly through our cultural bloodstream. Not the least important contrast between the ancients and ourselves is that in the ancient world celebrity retained its mystique as an indefeasibly inegalitarian commodity.

Principal Sources

Reference is made only to works cited in the text.

Ammianus Marcellinus (AD *c*. 330 – *c*. 395)
Commonly regarded as Rome's last great historian. Only his account of the period AD 353-378 survives.

Appian (AD *c*. 95 – *c*. 165)
An Egyptian Greek, whose *Roman History* ascribed Rome's success to her moderation, good sense, and virtue.

Athenaeus (early third century (AD))
An Egyptian Greek, who wrote an immensely learned encyclopaedic work called *Deipnosophistae* (*Sophists at Dinner*), valuable as a late source for the posthumous reputation of celebrities.

Aulus Gellius (AD *c*. 123 – *c*. 169)
Learned author of a miscellany of short essays on a wide variety of topics entitled *Noctes Atticae* (*Attic Nights*), written primarily for his children.

Cicero (106-43 BC)
Orator, politician, lawyer, and indefatigable correspondent, Cicero is our foremost witness for the final decades of the Roman Republic.

Diodorus Siculus (*c*. 80 – *c*. 29 BC)
Author of a universal history from mythological times to 60 BC, Diodorus is often condemned as dull and inaccurate.

Fronto (AD *c*. 100-166)
A rhetorician from Numidia (modern eastern Algeria), Fronto corresponded with the Emperors Marcus Aurelius and Lucius Verus.

Iamblichus (*c*. AD 245 – *c*. 325)
Author of what purports to be a compendium of Pythagorean philosophy, largely culled from earlier writers. It includes a *Life of Pythagoras*, indicative of the late blossoming interest in the sage.

Josephus (AD 37 – *c*. 100)
Jewish Pharisee, who became extremely pro-Roman. Author of the *Antiquitates Judaicae* (*Jewish Antiquities*).

Juvenal (AD *c*. 60 – *c*. 140)
Cantankerous author of sixteen *Satires* charged with moral indignation about the evils of his age.

Livy (59 BC – AD 17)
Author of a historical work in 142 books entitled *Ab urbe condita* (*From the Foundation of Rome*), which covered the period from the Trojan War to 9 BC. Only 25 books are extant.

Lucan (AD 39-65)
Author of an epic poem entitled *De bello civili* (*The Civil War*), which

throws an interesting light upon the posthumous reputation of Julius Caesar in the reign of Nero.

Lucian (born *c.* AD 120)
Essayist, satirist, wit and accomplished raconteur, whose attack on the 'false prophet' Alexander exposes all the characteristics of the quintessential religious virtuoso 'on the make'.

Lucretius (first half of first century BC).
Author of *De rerum natura* (*On the Nature of Things*), an epic poem which sets out the principles of Epicurean philosophy.

Martial (*c.* AD 38-101)
Author of twelve books of epigrams (some 1,175 poems in all), which relate gossip about the minor and major celebrities of his day.

Nepos (*c.* 110-24 BC)
The first biographer to write in Latin, recently described as 'an intellectual pygmy'.

Pausanias (*fl. c.* AD 150)
Greek travel writer, whose *Description of Greece*, published in AD 174, provides a highly useful account of the monuments of famous people that were visible in his day.

Philostratus (born *c.* AD 170)
Author of *Vitae sophistarum* (*Lives of the Sophists*), the most valuable work for our knowledge of the period known as the Second Sophistic, when professorial reputations depended on the ability to declaim in public.

Photius (AD *c.* 810 – *c.* 893)
Author of a work entitled *Bibliotheca* (*Library*), which, despite its many shortcomings, is our best source for many lost works from classical antiquity.

Pindar (born *c.* 518 BC)
Archaic Greece's most celebrated poet and the author of numerous odes commemorating the victories of his wealthy patrons in the major games.

Plato (*c.* 429-347 BC)
Author of the *Symposium*, which sheds an interesting light upon the effect of Socrates' charismatic personality on his 'star' pupil Alcibiades.

Pliny the Elder (AD 23-79)
Author of the *Natural History*, which allegedly contains twenty thousand facts, many having to do with art and architecture.

Pliny the Younger (AD 61 – *c.* 114)
Nephew and adopted son of Pliny the Elder, whose correspondence provides a valuable aside on his minor celebrity.

Plutarch (AD *c.* 46 – *c.* 126)
Author of *Parallel Lives*, fifty biographies of eminent Greek and Roman soldiers and statesmen, arranged in pairs. Plutarch is one of our foremost sources, alert as he is to the attention-seeking strategies of his subjects.

Porphyry (AD 234 – *c.* 305)
Author of a *Life of Pythagoras*, an excerpt from a longer work on the history of philosophy.

Procopius of Caesarea (born *c.* AD 500)
Author of the *Secret History*, memorable for its scurrilous attack on the Empress Theodora.

Principal Sources

St Augustine (AD 354-430)
   The pioneer in confessional literature.
Sallust (86-35 BC)
   Author of the *Bellum Catilinae* (*Catilinarian Conspiracy*) (published *c.* 42 BC), which, typical of the conservative Roman viewpoint, brandishes high-profile women as sluts.
Strabo (*c.* 64 BC – *c.* AD 21)
   Author of the *Geography*, a work of broader interest than its title suggests, which contains much information on political and economic history.
Suetonius (AD *c.* 69 – *c.* 150)
   Author of the *De viris illustribus* (*Lives of Illustrious Men*), biographies of Roman grammarians, poets, philosophers, and other men of letters, and of the *De vita Caesarum* (*Lives of the Twelve Caesars*), a work sometimes condemned for its relish for backstairs gossip but highly valuable for the study of imperial celebrity for that very reason.
Tacitus (AD *c.* 55-120)
   Author of the *Annals*, which cover the years AD 14-68, and of the *Histories*, which cover the years 69-96. Indisputably Rome's greatest historian, Tacitus is particularly valuable both for his depiction of the role of entertainers and for his characterization of the Emperor Tiberius.
Valerius Maximus (reign of Tiberius)
   Author of a promisingly entitled but lacklustre miscellany of illustrative examples entitled *Memorable Deeds and Sayings*.
Velleius Paterculus (born *c.* 20 BC)
   Author of the *Compendium of Roman History*, which moves at great speed through the entirety of Roman history in two books. The work is rhetorical and heavily pro-establishment in its presentation of the Principate, particularly in regard to the reign of Tiberius.
Xenophon (*c.* 428-354 BC)
   Author of the *Apology*, an account of Socrates' defence at his trial, and of the *Memoirs of Socrates*, which presents a far more down-to-earth picture of Socrates than that provided by Plato in his dialogues.

Time-Line

The conventional divisions:

c. 700-480 BC	Archaic Period
480-323 BC	Classical Period
323-31 BC	Hellenistic Period
510-27 BC	Republican Period
c. 133-27 BC	Late Republican Period
27 BC – AD 337	Imperial Period
337-565 AD	Late Imperial Period (also known as Late Antiquity)

BC

776	Coroebus of Elis wins the footrace at Olympia
c. 570	Birth of Pythagoras
544	Praxidamas of Aegina becomes the first Olympic victor to erect a statue at Olympia
c. 530	Pythagoras founds a sect in Croton
c. 500	Milo of Croton wins his sixth Olympic crown
c. 498	Pindar composes his first victory ode
490	Midas of Acragas wins the crown for *aulos*-playing at the Pythian Games
c. 480	Themistocles establishes a cult of Artemis Aristoboule ('Of the first-rate advice')
476	Aeschylus is invited to Syracuse by Hieron I
c. 444	Possible date of Protagoras' first visit to Athens
423	Socrates features as a major character in Aristophanes' *Clouds*
407	Alcibiades receives a hero's welcome in Athens
c. 404	The Spartan admiral Lysander is awarded divine honours
399	Trial and execution of Socrates
396	Cynisca of Sparta becomes the first woman to win the four-horse chariot race at Olympia
386	A contest in 'old' drama is introduced at the City Dionysia in Athens, thereby encouraging actors to develop their own repertoires
356	Herostratus burns down the temple of Artemis at Ephesus
338	Philip II of Macedon begins building the Philippeion at Olympia
331	Alexander the Great founds Alexandria in Egypt; visits oracle of Ammon at Siwah
328/7	Alexander demands formal obeisance from the Greeks and Macedonians in his army
321	Ptolemy I Soter kidnaps Alexander's corpse

153

279	Ptolemy II Philadelphus holds a magnificent festival known as the Ptolemaieia in Alexandria
c. 265	Arsinoë and Ptolemy II become 'brother-sister gods'
155	Delegation of Greek philosophers draws the crowds when it visits Rome and addresses the Senate
63	Orbilius begins his teaching career
c. 62	Death of the comic actor Roscius
66	Julius Caesar stages a gladiatorial contest to promote his visibility
55	The first stone theatre is erected in Rome by Pompey the Great
49-45	Pompey the Great and Caesar fight the Civil War
47	Birth of Cleopatra's son Caesarion
45	Caesar celebrates his quadruple triumph
42	Caesar is deified; Octavian assumes the title *divi filius* (son of the deified)
41	Cleopatra upstages Mark Antony at Tarsus
34	Cleopatra and Antony celebrate the 'Donations of Alexandria', the only Roman triumph to be conducted outside Rome
c. 33?	Octavian plans a colossal tomb in the Campus Martius known as the Mausoleum
31	Death of Cleopatra
29	Octavian celebrates his triple triumph
27	Octavian establishes the Principate and takes the title 'Augustus'
19	Augustus is mobbed on his return to Italy from the East
17	Augustus celebrates the tenth anniversary of the Principate

AD

14-16	Tiberius issues coins honouring Livia as 'Mother of the World'
19	Germanicus rebukes the Alexandrians for their tumultuous reception of him in Egypt
29	Fearful of her influence and popularity, Tiberius banishes Germanicus' widow the Elder Agrippina
60-230	Declamation becomes the most prestigious and popular form of literary activity in the period known as the Second Sophistic
66	Nero wins the Olympic crown for the chariot-race
107	Trajan orders 123 days of celebrations throughout the Empire to celebrate his victory over the Dacians
146	Inscription set up to commemorate the career of Caius Apuleius Diocles, 'the champion of all charioteers'
162	Galen begins practising medicine in Rome
212	Caracalla decrees that Roman citizens who enter the theatrical profession will be categorized as '*infames*' (without honour)
324	Constantine the Great confers the title 'Augusta' on his mother Helena
c. 360	Simeon the Stylite takes up residence on a pillar in the Syrian desert
c. 400	St Augustine publishes the first confessional autobiography
415	Murder of the mathematician Hypatia
527	Theodora becomes Empress of the Byzantine world

Coinage

Greek

100 *drachmas* = 1 *mina*
60 *minas* = 1 *talent*
An unskilled worker earned half a *drachma* in the second half of the
fifth century BC, and one and a half *drachmas* in the late fourth
century.

Roman

4 *sestertii* = 1 *denarius*
25 *denarii* = 1 *aureus*
In Julius Caesar's day a legionary earned about two hundred *denarii* a year.
A century later the figure had risen to about nine hundred *denarii* a year.

Notes

Introduction

1. J. Campbell, *The Power of Myth* (New York 1988: 163).
2. Homer *Odyssey* 11.489-91.
3. Vergil *Aeneid* 2.588ff.
4. Cicero *Tusculan Disputations* 5.16.46; cf. *De republica* 6.19-21.
5. Pliny the Younger *Letters* 9.23.2-5, citing the delight which the famous Attic orator Demosthenes experienced when he was recognized by a woman carrying water (cf. Cicero *Tusculan Disputations* 5.103).
6. Plutarch *Pompey* 23.3.
7. Valerius Maximus 3.4.
8. Strabo 14.1.22, Cicero *De natura deorum* 1.23.47, Valerius Maximus 8.14, etc.
9. The phenomenon of the suicide bomber who is motivated by a desire for self-glorification has recently been dubbed 'the Herostratus syndrome'. See A. Borowitz, *Terrorism for Self-Glorification* (Kent State University Press 2005).
10. Diodorus Siculus 16.94.1. Pausanias' motives for killing Philip may have been rather more complex, since the king had forbidden him to revenge himself on a man who had sexually humiliated him (Aristotle *Politics* 5.1311b1-3).
11. Lucretius 3.75-8. Horace *Satires* 1.6 also delivers a scathing attack on those who seek political or social advancement.
12. Suetonius *Augustus* 99.1.
13. Valerius Maximus' *Memorable Deeds and Sayings* is of little value. Lost treatises that may have touched on the subject of celebrity include Amphicrates' *On Famous Men* and Cicero's *On Glory*.

1. The Media Tart

1. Homer *Odyssey* 8.74, cf. 9.20.
2. Herodotus 1.60.4-6. See Lavelle (2004) for a detailed investigation of Pisistratus' courting of fame as a stepping stone in his path to power.
3. See Frost (1981: 37) for further discussion of aristocratic competitiveness.
4. Plutarch *Cimon* 10.5 tells of a Spartan aristocrat named Lichas, who won renown throughout Greece by hosting lavish dinner parties for foreigners at the festival of the Gymnopaidia.
5. Plutarch *Themistocles* 22.1-2. For the cult see R.S.J. Garland, *Introducing New Gods* (London and Ithaca 1992: ch. 3).
6. Plutarch *Cimon* 10.

7. Plutarch *Cimon* 8.6.
8. Plutarch *Nicias* 5.2. See further Rhodes (2004: 192-5).
9. For details of the statues, see Stewart (1993: 55).
10. Plutarch *Aristides* 7.5-6. Ostracism was in a very real sense the price that celebrities paid for being famous in democratic Athens. It seems to have been introduced precisely for the purpose of cutting down to size those who overstepped the bounds of moderation and whose reputations threatened to overwhelm their rivals.
11. Nepos *Alcibiades* 7.
12. Plutarch *Alcibiades* 24.4.
13. Aristophanes *Frogs* 1425.
14. Plutarch *Alcibiades* 9.
15. Plutarch *Alcibiades* 23.4.
16. Plutarch *Alcibiades* 23.3.
17. Plutarch *Alcibiades* 23.7. I owe this observation to Paul Cartledge.
18. Plutarch *Alcibiades* 32.1.
19. M. Orth, *The Importance of Being Famous: Behind the Scenes of the Celebrity-Industrial Complex* (New York 2004: 25).
20. Thucydides 6.15.
21. Cartledge (2005: 240f.), Rhodes (2006: 378).
22. Plutarch *Cimon* 8.1. Only the Spartan king Agesilaus II, it is alleged, had the tact, or perhaps the good sense, to decline the offer of divine honours.
23. Pausanias 1.18.3, who adds that Themistocles' name had been erased and replaced by that of a Thracian. See further Zanker (1995: 63-5).
24. Cicero *De amicitia* 12.42.
25. Plutarch *Moralia* 869c; cf. *Themistocles* 7.
26. Richter (1984: 169).
27. Plutarch *Themistocles* 32.3.
28. Plato *Gorgias* 518e-519b.
29. Nepos *Alcibiades* 11.
30. Valerius Maximus 3.1 ext. 1.
31. Persius *Satires* 4.3ff.
32. Pliny the Elder *Natural History* 34.26.
33. Richter (1984: 81-3).

2. The Royal Icon

1. Plutarch *Alexander* 4.5.
2. Pausanias 5.20.9f.
3. Diodorus Siculus 16.8.6.
4. Plutarch *Moralia* 328.
5. The conservative view is that of Fraser (1996).
6. For other examples of 'heroic imitation', see Hornblower (2002: 290).
7. For contemporary portraits of Alexander, see Stewart (1993: 52f.).
8. The testimonia regarding Alexander's appearance are provided by Stewart (op. cit.: 341-50).
9. For the Porus coinage, see Stewart (op. cit.: 201-6).
10. Alexander's head has also been recognized on two coins that were issued in Egypt in *c.* 330 BC, though the identification is far from certain.

11. *Fragmente der griechischen Historiker* 124. Had Callisthenes' work survived, it would have stood interesting comparison with Julius Caesar's carefully crafted *Commentaries* (see p. 43). For an ancient verdict on Choerilus of Iasus, see Horace (*Letters* 2.1.232-4), who talks of his 'crude and ill-begotten verses'.

12. Cartledge (2005: 289-94) and Tarn (in Griffith 1966: 151-63).

13. Diodorus Siculus 16.92.5.

14. Cartledge (op. cit.: ch. 11).

15. Plutarch *Alexander* 2.1-3.2.

16. See Stewart (op. cit.: Appendix 3) for a full list of cults established in Alexander's name.

17. Suetonius *Augustus* 18.1.

18. Pliny the Elder *Natural History* 35.93-4.

19. Livy 9.17-19.

20. Appian *Civil Wars* 2.149-54.

21. Seneca *Natural Questions* 6.23.3.

22. Aulus Gellius 7.8.3.

3. The Consummate Populist

1. Caesar *Civil War* 1.9.2. Cf. Cicero *Partitiones oratoriae* 90, where '*dignitas*' is equated with 'distinction, honour, glory, fidelity, justice, and all forms of virtue'.

2. Plutarch *Caesar* 2.

3. Suetonius *Julius* 32.

4. Polybius 10.11.5-8. See F.W. Walbank, 'The Scipionic legend', in *Selected Papers: Studies in Greek and Roman History and Historiography* (Cambridge 1985: 120-37, esp. 134f.).

5. Scholars are deeply divided as to whether something akin to democracy prevailed in Late Republican Rome. One of the leading advocates of the view that it did is Millar (1998: esp. 197-226). For a contrary opinion, see Mouritsen (2001: esp. 128-48). Though the *comitia centuriata*, which held the consular elections, favoured the wealthy, Phillips (2004: 56) argues that the plebs did occasionally decide their outcome. (Voter turnout at such elections is generally put at between fifty-five thousand and seventy thousand.) Yavetz's observation (1969: 39) that 'Democracy did not exist in Rome, but popular pressure did' comes close to my own line of reasoning.

6. Valerius Maximus 3.6.

7. Pliny the Elder *Natural History* 36.41, Suetonius *Nero* 46.1. See in general D. Sudjic, *The Edifice Complex: How the Rich and Powerful Shape the World* (Harmondsworth and London 2005).

8. Westall (1996: 83-118) discusses the political implications of the Julian Forum. Ancient sources include Pliny the Elder *Natural History* 36.103.

9. Pliny the Elder *Natural History* 34.30.

10. Dio 44.4-5. For the portraits, see Toynbee (1978: 30f.).

11. Pliny the Elder *Natural History* 7.91-2.

4. The Imperial Superstar

1. The last person not a member of the imperial family to be awarded a triumph was Lucius Cornelius Balbus in 19 BC.
2. Suetonius *Augustus* 43.1.
3. On acclamations, see Aldrete (1999: esp. 101-5).
4. Fronto in Loeb edn (Cambridge, MA and London 1982: vol. 1, p. 206f.).
5. *Res Gestae* 11, Dio 54.10. Other emperors who were greeted by enthusiastic crowds on their return from abroad include Nero, Vespasian, Trajan and Commodus. See Aldrete (1999: 112f.).
6. Suetonius *Augustus* 98.2.
7. Vergil *Eclogues* 1.6, *Georgics* 1.498ff.
8. Horace *Odes* 1.2.25ff.
9. Suetonius *Augustus* 52.
10. For the target audience of the *Res Gestae* see Yavetz (1984: 14-20).
11. Suetonius *Tiberius* 26.2.
12. A.S. Hunt and C.C. Edgar, *Select Papyri* (Cambridge, MA and London: vol. 2 no. 211).
13. Suetonius *Tiberius* 21.3.

5. The Sports Star

1. Homer *Odyssey* 8.146-8; cf. 8.100-3.
2. Herodotus 3.137.5.
3. Pausanias 6.11.2.
4. Pindar *Olympian ode* 7.81-7, with note in Loeb edn of Pindar (London and New York 1919: 69).
5. Pindar *Pythian ode* 3.70-2.
6. *Inscriptiones Graecae* XIV.1102.
7. Pindar *Olympian ode* 1.97-9.
8. *Inscriptiones Graecae* VII.1888b.
9. Young (2004: 113).
10. Pliny the Elder *Natural History* 7.186.
11. *Corpus Inscriptionum Latinarum* 6.10,048. N. Lewis and M. Reinhold, *Roman Civilization*, vol. 2: *The Empire* (3rd edn, New York 1990: 146 n. 16), point out that this comes to 'an average of 177 races a year ... or an average of three to four races on each of the fifty circus days of the year'.
12. *Corpus Inscriptionum Latinarum* 6.10,047. The observation, drawn from Suetonius *De grammaticis* 17.2, is that of Ewigleben (2000: 134).
13. *Historia Augusta: Elagabalus* 6. Cf. A. Cameron, *Porphyrius the Charioteer* (Oxford 1973: 250-2).
14. Cassiodorus, *Variae* 3.51 (tr. H.A. Harris, *Sport in Greece and Rome* [London 1972] 230f.).
15. Suetonius *Nero* 53.
16. Suetonius *Nero* 20.3.
17. Tacitus *Annals* 14.15.
18. Tacitus *Annals* 16.5.
19. Suetonius *Nero* 21.3.
20. Suetonius *Nero* 23.2-3; Tacitus *Annals* 16.4.

21. See further C.E. Manning, 'Acting and Nero's conception of the principate', *Greece and Rome* 22 (1975) 164-75.

22. Diodorus Siculus 12.9, Strabo *Geography* 6.1.12, Athenaeus *Deipnosophistae* 10.412ef. For other feats by Milo, see Pausanias 6.14.5-8, Philostratus *Vita Apollonii* 4.28, Aelian *Varia historia* 12.22.

23. Cicero *Tusculan Disputations* 1.46.111.

24. Pausanias 6.11.9. See Miller (2004: 164).

25. Pausanias 6.9.6-8.

26. Tacitus *Historia* 2.8-9, Dio 66.19.3, Suetonius *Nero* 57.2. See P.A. Gallivan, 'The false Neros: a re-examination', in *Historia* 22 (1973) 364-5, for discussion of the number of impostors.

27. Plutarch *Moralia* 567f. R.M. Frazer, Jr, 'Nero, the singing animal', pp. 215-18 in *Arethusa* 4 (1971), suggests that the metamorphosis into a frog is probably an allusion to the tone of Nero's voice.

6. The Celebrity Guru

1. Homer *Odyssey* 17.382-5.

2. S. Collini, *Absent Minds: Intellectuals in Britain* (Oxford 2006: 481f.). As Collini notes, Huxley's posthumous reputation was considerably enhanced by the inclusion of his face on the sleeve of the Beatles' 'Sergeant Pepper' album.

3. Plato *Protagoras* 315a.

4. Plato *Hippias maior* 282e.

5. Plato *Apology* 18b-19d.

6. Plato *Symposium* 215e.

7. Plutarch *Alexander* 14; Valerius Maximus 4 ext. 4a.

8. Herodotus 1.24. See S. Flory, 'Brave gestures in Herodotus', in *American Journal of Philology* 99 (1978) 411-21.

9. Lucian, *Herodotus or Aëtion*; cf. Suda *s.v.* Thucydides.

10. Suetonius *Life of Vergil* 11. Horace *Satires* 1.9 treats of another hazard confronting those in the limelight: the hanger-on, who attaches himself to their circle in the hope of achieving the celebrity so far denied him.

11. Pliny the Younger *Letters* 4.19.2.

12. See J. O'Donnell, 'Augustine: his time and lives', in E. Stump and N. Kretzmann, *The Cambridge Guide to Augustine* (Cambridge 2001: 12f.).

13. Pliny the Elder *Natural History* 35.20; Plutarch *Pericles* 2.1.

14. Vergil *Aeneid* 6.847-53.

15. Suetonius *De grammaticis* 9.

16. Philostratus *Lives of the Sophists* 2.10 (587).

17. *Philostratus and Eunapius: Lives of the Sophists* (Loeb Classical Library [London and Cambridge 1921]) xv. Wright continues (xvi): 'A successful sophist must have the nerve and equipment of a great actor, since he must act character parts ... he must have unusual charm of appearance, manner, and voice, and a ready wit to retort to his rivals.' For the idolizing of educators by Roman youths, see further Eyben (1993: 222-30).

18. Augustine *Confessions* 4.14.

19. Diogenes Laertius 2.38-9.

20. Aeschines 1.173.

21. Plutarch *Cato* 23.1.

22. Cicero *Tusculan Disputations* 5.4.10.

23. Valerius Maximus 3.4 ext. 1.

24. Fronto in Loeb edn (Cambridge, MA and London 1982: vol. I, pp. 100-3).

25. For the afterlife of the tragedians, see R.S.J. Garland, *Surviving Greek Tragedy* (London 2004: 5-11).

26. Aulus Gellius 8.4.

7. The Religious Charismatic

1. Latterday charismatics include Charles Manson, who convinced his followers to murder ten innocent people; and the Rev. Jim Jones, founder of a commune known as the People's Temple in the jungle of Guyana, who induced hundreds of his followers to commit suicide. (As in the *Bacchae*, the latter agreed to do so in order to merge their identity with their leader, whom they regarded as a living god.)

2. E. Rohde, *Psyche: The Cult of Souls and Belief in Immortality among the Ancient Greeks*, 8th edn, trans. W.B. Hillis (London and New York 1925: 374).

3. Porphyry *Pythagoras* 18.

4. Luke 10:1, 5.

5. The belief that Jesus shared much in common with pagan virtuosi inspired a notorious footnote by Edward Gibbon in *Decline and Fall of the Roman Empire*. In reference to the Cappadocian mystic who is the subject of a romantic and largely fictional biography by Philostratus (*c.* AD 218), Gibbon writes (vol. 1, ch. 11): 'Apollonius of Tyana was born about the same time as Jesus Christ. His life (that of the former) is related in so fabulous a manner by his fanatic disciples, that we are at a loss to discover whether he was a sage, an impostor, or a fanatic.' The finessing parenthesis notwithstanding, Gibbon's heretical undertone is inescapable.

6. Acts 8:9-24.

7. As Fredriksen (2000: 104) notes, crucifixion was customarily reserved for political prisoners. In addition, the fact that the Gospels were written after the failure of the First Jewish Revolt (AD 66-70) made it prudent to eliminate any political overtones that Jesus' message might originally have held for his contemporaries.

8. Matthew 10:17-19; Mark 13:9-13; Luke 21:12-19.

9. Lucian *Alexander* 4.

10. Lucian *Alexander* 13.

11. For an account of Simeon's life, see Doran (1992: 15-66).

12. Pliny the Elder *Natural History* 34.26. See M. Griffin in *Cambridge Ancient History*, 2nd edn, vol. IX (Cambridge 1994: 707-10).

13. Pliny the Elder *Natural History* 35.160.

14. E.g. Lucian *Alexander* 4.

15. Josephus *Jewish Antiquities* 18.63-64. His praenomen 'Flavius' indicates that Josephus took the name of his patron, the Emperor Flavius Vespasianus, when he became a Roman citizen.

16. Tacitus *Annals* 15.44. A reference to 'Chrestus' in Suetonius *Claudius* 25 may either be to Jesus or to another Jewish leader of that name.

17. Evagrius Scholasticus *Ecclesiastical History* 1.13.

18. For a comprehensive list of stylites throughout history, see Pena (1991: Appendix 2).

8. The Showbiz Star

1. Augustine *Confessions* 4.14.
2. Xenophon *Symposium* 3.6.
3. Plato *Ion* 535d.
4. Scholion on Sophocles *Ajax* 864.
5. Aristotle *Politics* 7.1336b28-31.
6. Aulus Gellius 6.5.
7. Naples, Nat. Mus. no. 9019. See Easterling (2002: 328-31, with Fig. 58).
8. Tacitus *Annals* 16.4.
9. [Plutarch] *Moralia* 848b, Aulus Gellius 11.9.2. See Lightfoot (2002: 213-15).
10. Aristophanes *Knights* 1278, cf. *Wasps* 1278.
11. Wilson (2002: 53).
12. Athenaeus *Deipnosophistae* 13.577c (Lamia) and 597a (Nanno).
13. Plutarch *Brutus* 21.6.
14. Pliny the Elder *Natural History* 7.128. For Roscius' career, see Fantham (2002: 364-7). Sulla may have hoped that some of the popularity of his actor friends would rub off on him so that he would achieve what Alan Shroeder, author of *How Show Business Took Over the White House* (Boulder 2004), has mischievously dubbed 'gilt by association'.
15. Plutarch *Sulla* 36.1.
16. Tacitus *Annals* 1.77.
17. Levick (1983: 97-115).
18. For the two types of entertainers, see Potter (1999: 273-6).
19. *Inscriptiones Graecae* XIV 2342 = Csapo and Slater (1995: ch. 5, no. 18). See Webb (2002: 301f.).
20. Tacitus *Annals* 1.77 (identified separately from the actors in n. 16 above).
21. Csapo and Slater (1995: ch. 5, no. 36).
22. Augustine *Confessions* 6.8. Cf. Epictetus *Enchiridion* 33.2. For the popular appeal of gladiators see Hopkins (1983: 20-7) and Kyle (1998: 2-4).
23. Petronius *Satyricon* 52.3; 71.6-9.
24. Martial 5.24.
25. *Corpus Inscriptionum Latinarum* 4.4397, 4356.
26. Juvenal *Satires* 6.103-13.
27. Suetonius *Tiberius* 7.1; *Nero* 30.2.
28. Stobaeus *Florilegium* 4.34.70, 4.33.28.
29. Aulus Gellius 5.8.4.
30. Tacitus *Annals* 15.46.
31. Frontinus *Strategemata* 1.5.20-2; 1.7.6; 2.5.34.

9. The Sexually Liberated Female

1. Thucydides 2.45.2. According to his wife Ludmila, President Putin sees

163

eye-to-eye with Pericles. She claims that her husband has two golden rules: 'A woman must do everything in the home' and 'You should not praise a woman – otherwise you will spoil her' (*Guardian Weekly* 17-23 June 2005).

2. The issue, of course, is very much alive today. An advertisement in *The Independent* (20 July 2005) began: 'In the post-feminist age of ladettes and girl power, are women now more free to think innovatively and express their creativity, or are they still constrained by old stereotypes? More than 130 years after Mary Ann Evans felt she had to use the male pseudonym George Eliot to publish *Middlemarch*, many believe women's potential for creativity is finally being unleashed. But an alternative view suggests that today's upfront women may really be following an agenda set by men.'

3. Pliny the Elder *Natural History* 36.20.

4. Herodotus 2.134-5. As 'Rhodopis' translates 'Rosy Cheeks', this was probably her professional name. For other colourful nicknames applied to *hetaerae* see McClure (2003: 68-74).

5. Aulus Gellius 1.8.

6. The incident of Phryne's disrobing is described in Athenaeus *Deipnosophistae* 13.590de, [Plutarch] *Moralia* 849de, and Sextus Empiricus *Against the Mathematicians* 2.4. There is an excellent discussion of Phryne in McClure (2003: 126-36).

7. E.G. Turner, 'Ptolemaic Egypt', in *Cambridge Ancient History*, 2nd edn, vol. VII.1 (Cambridge 1985: 136-8).

8. Plutarch *Tiberius Gracchus* 1. See Petrocelli (2001: 34-65).

9. Pliny the Elder *Natural History* 31.120; Valerius Maximus 8.15.12.

10. *Corpus Inscriptionum Latinarum* 6.1527. Translated by J. Shelton in *As the Romans Did* (2nd edn, Oxford 1998: 292-4).

11. See further Fraschetti (2001a: 100-17).

12. Sallust *Catilinarian Conspiracy* 25.

13. Tacitus *Annals* 3.4.

14. Bauman (1992: 168). For the difficulty in disentangling the sexual from the political in Tacitus' narrative, see S.R. Joshel, 'Female desire and the discourse of empire: Tacitus' Messalina', in Hallett and Skinner (1997: 221-54).

15. Pliny the Elder *Natural History* 10.172.

16. Socrates Scholasticus *Ecclesiastical History* 6.15. For discussion of Hypatia's complex identity, see J.M. Rist, 'Hypatia', in *Phoenix* 19 (1965: 214-25) and Ronchey (2001: 160-89).

17. Valerius Maximus 4.3 ext. 3a.

18. Pausanias 10.15.1. Similarly Alexander the Great's shady finance minister Harpalus is said to have set up a statue of his mistress Glycera in Rhosus, Syria – at the exact spot where he proposed to erect statues of Alexander and himself (Athenaeus *Deipnosophistae* 13.595d).

19. Seneca *Dialogi* 12.16.6, Tacitus *Dialogus* 28.5-6, Valerius Maximus 4.4 *praef.*

20. Pliny the Elder *Natural History* 34.31.

21. *Patrologia Latina* 25.1337C.

22. Juvenal 6.114-32.

23. John of Nikiû *Chronicle* 84.87-103.

10. The Tabloid Queen

1. See Goudchaux (2001: 210-14) for the coin portraits.

2. For possible sculptural portraits, see Walker (2001: 142-7), and Walker and Ashton (2006, forthcoming). The Egyptian reliefs of Cleopatra, such as the one on the temple of Hathor at Dendera (Walker and Higgs 2001: 138[top]), can hardly be considered portraits.

3. Plutarch *Antonius* 27.2-3.

4. Plutarch *Antonius* 26.1-3.

5. Plutarch *Antonius* 62.1.

6. Horace *Odes* 1.37, as discussed on p. 140 above. The suggestion that the story of Cleopatra's suicide may have been fabricated by Octavian was advanced in a documentary entitled 'Who Killed Cleopatra?' by Atlantic Productions (2004).

7. Procopius *Secret History* 9.12.

8. Procopius *Secret History* 9.21. Edward Gibbon, *The History of the Decline and Fall of the Roman Empire* (vol. 5, ch. 40), was hardly less salacious, observing that Theodora's 'venal charms were abandoned to a promiscuous crowd of citizens and strangers' – a roundabout way of describing her as a nymphomaniac. He also eloquently paraphrased Procopius to the effect that 'after exhausting the arts of sensual pleasure, she most ungratefully murmured against the parsimony of Nature' – for not providing her with an extra orifice!

9. Procopius *Wars* 1.24.36-7.

10. See Connor (2004: 133-45) for a detailed description of the portrait.

11. Procopius *Buildings* 1.11.8-9.

12. Propertius 3.11.30, 39.

13. Horace *Odes* 1.37.

14. BM GR 1865.11-18.249 = Walker and Higgs (2001, fig. 357 [p. 337]).

15. Plutarch *Antonius* 86.5.

16. Dio 51.22-3.

17. Ammianus Marcellinus 28.4.6 (most probably a reference to Cleopatra VII). See Grant (1972, 233) for further references to Cleopatra's posthumous reputation.

18. Procopius *Buildings* 4.7.5.

Conclusions

1. *Corpus Inscriptionum Latinarum* 4, with suppl. 2 and 3.

2. Valerius Maximus 3.4.

Bibliography

Introduction

Allport, G.W., and Postman, L. (1954) *The Basic Psychology of Rumour in Public Opinion and Propaganda*. New York.

Boorstin, D. (1961) *The Image: A Guide to Pseudo-Events in America*. New York.

Braudy, L. (1986) *The Frenzy of Renown: Fame and its History*. Oxford and New York.

Collini, S. (2006) 'Long views II: authority to celebrity', pp. 473-98 in *Absent Minds: Intellectuals in Britain*. Oxford.

Goffman, E. (1959) *The Presentation of Self in Everyday Life*. New York.

Lindholm, C. (1990) *Charisma*. Oxford.

Marshall, D.P. (1997) *Celebrity and Power: Fame in Contemporary Culture*. Minneapolis.

Orth, M. (2004) *The Importance of Being Famous: Behind the Scenes of the Celebrity-Industrial Complex*. New York.

Suls, J., ed. (1982) *Psychological Perspectives on Self and Identity*, vol. 1. Washington, D.C.

1. The Media Tart

Cartledge, P. (2005) *Alexander the Great: The Hunt for a New Past*, rev. edn. London and New York.

Davies, J.K. (1981) *Wealth and the Power of Wealth in Classical Athens*. New York.

Finley, M.I. (2004) 'Athenian demagogues', pp. 163-84 in P.J. Rhodes, ed., *Athenian Democracy*. Oxford. First published in *Past and Present* 21 (1962) 3-24. Revised version in M.I. Finley, *Democracy Ancient and Modern*, 2nd edn, pp. 38-75. London and Rutgers 1985.

Frost, F.J. (1981) 'Politics in early Athens,' pp. 33-9 in *Classical Contributions: Studies in Honour of M.F. McGregor*. Locust Valley.

Hughes-Hallett, L. (2004) *Heroes: Saviours, Traitors and Supermen*. London and New York.

Lavelle, B.M. (2004) *Fame, Money, and Power: The Rise of Peisistratos and 'Democratic' Tyranny at Athens*. Ann Arbor.

Rhodes, P.J. (2004) 'Political activity in classical Athens', pp. 185-206 in P.J. Rhodes, ed., *Athenian Democracy*. Oxford. First published in *Journal of Hellenic Studies* 106 (1986) 132-44.

Rhodes, P.J. (2006) *A History of the Classical Greek World 478-323 BC*. Oxford.

Richter, G.M.A. (1984) *The Portraits of the Greeks*, rev. by R.R.R. Smith. Ithaca, NY.
Stewart, A. (1993) *Faces of Power: Alexander's Image and Hellenistic Politics*. Berkeley, etc.
Zanker, P. (1995) *The Mask of Socrates: The Image of the Intellectual in Antiquity*, trans. A. Shapiro. Berkeley.

2. The Royal Icon

Bieber, M. (1964) *Alexander the Great in Greek and Roman Art*. Chicago.
Bosworth, A.B., and Baynham, E.J., eds (2000) *Alexander the Great in Fact and Fiction*. Oxford.
Cartledge, P. (2005) *Alexander the Great: The Hunt for a New Past*, rev. edn. London and New York.
Fraser, P.M. (1996) *The Cities of Alexander the Great*. Oxford.
Griffith, G.T., ed. (1966) *Alexander the Great: The Main Problems*. Cambridge and New York.
Hornblower, S. (2002) *The Greek World, 479-323 BC*, 3rd edn. London and New York.
Pearson, L. (1960) *Lost Histories of Alexander*. Chico, CA (reprint 1980).
Spencer, D. (2002) *Roman Alexander: Reading a Cultural Myth*. Exeter.
Stewart, A. (1993) *Faces of Power: Alexander's Image and Hellenistic Politics*. Berkeley, etc.
Tarn, W.W. (1948) *Alexander the Great*, 2 vols. Cambridge.

3. The Consummate Populist

Garland, R.S.J. (2003) *Julius Caesar*. Bristol.
Gelzer, M. (1969) *Caesar: Politician and Statesman*, trans. of 6th German edn (1959) first published in 1921. Oxford.
Millar, F.G.B. (1998) *The Crowd in Rome in the Late Republic*. Ann Arbor.
Mouritsen, H. (2001) *Plebs and Politics in the Late Roman Republic*. Cambridge.
Phillips, D.A. (2004) 'Voter turnout in consular elections', pp. 48-60 in *Ancient History Bulletin* 18.1-2.
Toynbee, J.M.C. (1978) *Roman Historical Portraits*. Ithaca, NY.
Westall, R. (1996) 'The Forum Iulium as representation of Imperator Caesar', pp. 83-118 in *Mitteilungen des deutschen archäologischen Instituts: Römische Abteilung* 103.
Weinstock, S. (1971) *Divus Julius*. Oxford.
Yavetz, Z. (1969) *Plebs and Princeps*. Oxford.

4. The Imperial Superstar

Aldrete, G.S. (1999) *Gestures and Acclamations in Ancient Rome*. Baltimore.
Brunt, P.A., and Moore, J.M. (1967) *Res Gestae Divi Augusti*. Oxford.
Millar, F.G.B., and Segal, E., eds (1984) *Caesar Augustus: Seven Aspects*. Oxford.

Bibliography

Raaflaub, K.A., and Toher, M., eds. (1990) *Between Republic and Empire: Interpretations of Augustus and his Empire*. Berkeley.

Taylor, L.R. (1931) *The Divinity of the Roman Emperor*. Philadelphia (reprinted 1975).

Walker S., and Burnett, A. (1981) *The Image of Augustus*. London.

Yavetz, Z. (1969) *Plebs and Princeps*. Oxford.

Yavetz, Z. (1984) 'The *Res Gestae* and Augustus' public image', pp. 1-36 in *Caesar Augustus: Seven Aspects*, ed. F. Millar and E. Segal. Oxford.

Zanker, P. (2001) *The Power of Images in the Age of Augustus*, trans. A. Shapiro. Ann Arbor.

5. The Sports Star

Golden, M. (1998) *Sport and Society in Ancient Greece*. Cambridge.

Humphrey, J.H. (1986) *Roman Circuses: Arenas for Chariot Racing*. Berkeley.

Miller, S.G. (2004) *Ancient Greek Athletics*. New Haven and London.

Spivey, N. (2004) *The Ancient Olympics: A History*. Oxford

Young, D. (2004) *A Brief History of the Olympic Games*. Oxford.

6. The Celebrity Guru

Cameron, A. (1965) 'Wandering poets', pp. 470-509 in *Historia* 14.

De Romilly, J. (1992) *The Great Sophists in Periclean Athens*, trans. J. Lloyd. Oxford.

Eyben, E. (1993) *Restless Youth in Ancient Rome*. London and New York.

Kerferd, G.B. (1981) *The Sophistic Movement*. Cambridge, etc.

Zanker, P. (1995) *The Mask of Socrates: The Image of the Intellectual in Antiquity*, trans. A. Shapiro. Berkeley.

7. The Religious Charismatic

Crossan, J.D. (1994) *Jesus: A Revolutionary Biography*. New York.

Doran, R. (1992) *The Lives of Symeon Stylites*. Kalamazoo.

Fredriksen, P. (2000) *From Jesus to Christ*, 2nd edn. New Haven and London.

Hadas, M., and Smith, M. (1965) *Heroes and Gods: Spiritual Biographies in Antiquity*. New York.

Pena, I. (1991) *The Amazing Life of the Syrian Monks in the Fourth to Sixth Centuries*. Milan.

Weber, M. (1946) *From Max Weber: Essays in Sociology*, ed. H. Gerth and C. Wright Mills. New York and Oxford.

Weber, M. (1963) *The Sociology of Religion*, 4th edn, trans. E. Fischoff. Boston.

8. The Showbiz Star

Cameron, A. (1976) *Circus Factions: Blues and Greens at Rome and Byzantium*. Oxford.

Chaniotis, A. (1990) ' Theatricality beyond the theatre: staging public life in the Hellenistic world', pp. 219-59 in *Pallas* 47.

Csapo, E., and Slater, W.J. (1995) *The Context of Ancient Drama*. Ann Arbor.

Daly, J. (1971) *An Actor in Rome*. London.

Easterling, P.E. (2002) 'Actor as icon', pp. pp. 327-41 in Easterling and Hall (2002).

Easterling P.E., and Hall, E., eds (2002) *Greek and Roman Actors: Aspects of an Ancient Profession*. Cambridge.

Fantham, E. (2002) 'Orator and/et actor', pp. 362-76 in Easterling and Hall (2002).

Garton, C. (1972) *Personal Aspects of the Roman Theatre*. Toronto.

Hopkins, K. (1983) *Death and Renewal*. Cambridge.

Hopkins, K., and Beard, M. (2005) *The Colosseum*. London.

Ewigleben, C., and Köhne, E., eds (2000) *Gladiators and Caesars: The Power of Spectacle in Ancient Rome*, English version edited by R. Jackson. Berkeley.

Kyle, D.G. (1998) *Spectacles of Death in Ancient Rome*. London and New York.

Levick, B. (1983) 'The senatus consultum from Larinum', pp. 97-115 in *Journal of Roman Studies* 73.

Lightfoot, J.L. (2002) 'Nothing to do with the *technitai* of Dionysus?', pp. 209-24 in Easterling and Hall (2002).

Potter, D.S. (1999) 'Entertainers in the Roman Empire', pp. 256-325 in D.S. Potter and D.J. Mattingly, eds, *Life, Death and Entertainment in the Roman Empire*. Ann Arbor

Scheithauer A. (1997) 'Les aulètes dans le théâtre grec à l'époque hellénistique', pp. 107-27 in *Pallas* 47.

Slater, N. (1990) 'The idea of the actor', pp. 385-95 in J.J. Winkler and F.I. Zeitlin, eds, *Nothing to Do with Dionysos? Athenian Drama in its Social Context*. Princeton.

Webb, R. (2002) 'Female entertainers in late antiquity', pp. 282-303 in Easterling and Hall (2002).

Wiedemann, T. (1992) *Emperors and Gladiators*. London and New York.

Wilson, P. (2002) 'The musicians among the actors', pp. 39-68 in Easterling and Hall (2002).

9. The Sexually Liberated Female

Balsdon, J.P.V.D. (1962) *Roman Women*. London.

Bauman, R. (1992) *Women and Politics in Ancient Rome*. London and New York.

Fantham, E., Foley, H.P., Kampen, N.B., Pomeroy, S.B., and Shapiro, H.A. (1995) *Women in the Classical World*. Oxford.

Fraschetti, A., ed. (2001) *Roman Women*, trans. L. Lappin. Chicago and London.

Fraschetti, A. (2001a) 'Livia the politician', pp. 100-17 in Fraschetti (2001).

Hallett, J.P., and Skinner, M.B., eds (1997) *Roman Sexualities*. Princeton.

Lefkowitz, M.R. (1983) 'Influential women', pp. 49-64 in A. Cameron and A. Kuhrt, eds, *Images of Women in Antiquity*, rev. edn 1993. London and Canberra.

McClure, L. (2003) *Courtesans at Table: Gender and Greek Literary Culture in Athenaeus*. London

Petrocelli, C. (2001) 'Cornelia the matron', pp. 34-65 in Fraschetti (2001).

Pomeroy, S.B. (1975) *Goddesses, Whores, Wives and Slaves: Women in Classical Antiquity*. New York.

Bibliography

10. The Tabloid Queen

Allen, P. (1992) 'Contemporary portrayals of the Byzantine Empress Theodora', pp. 93-102 in Garlick, B., Dixon, S., and Allen, P., *Stereotypes of Women in Power: Historical Perspectives and Revisionist Views*. New York.

Atwater, R. (1961) *Procopius: Secret History*, Foreword by A.E.R. Boak. Ann Arbor.

Browning, R. (1987) *Justinian and Theodora*, rev. edn. London.

Cameron, Averil (1985) *Procopius and the Sixth Century*. London.

Connor, C.L. (2004) *Women of Byzantium*. New Haven.

Evans, J.A.S. (2002) *The Empress Theodora: Partner of Justinian*. Austin.

Fisher, E.A. (1984) 'Theodora and Antonia in the *Historia Arcana*', pp. 287-313 in J. Peradotto and J.P. Sullivan, eds, *Women in the Ancient World: The Arethusa Papers*. Albany.

Goudchaux, G.W. (2001) 'Was Cleopatra beautiful? The conflicting answers of numismatics', pp. 210-14 in Walker and Higgs (2001).

Grant, M. (1972) *Cleopatra*. New York.

Hughes-Hallett, L. (1990) *Cleopatra: History, Dreams and Distortions*. New York.

Ronchey, S. (2001) 'Hypatia the intellectual', pp. 160-89 in A. Fraschetti, ed., *Roman Women*, trans. L. Lappin. Chicago and London.

Walker, S. (2001) 'Cleopatra's images: reflections of reality', pp. 142-47 in Walker and Higgs (2001).

Walker, S., and Ashton, S.-A. (2006, forthcoming) *Cleopatra*. London.

Walker, S., and Higgs, P. (2001) *Cleopatra of Egypt: From History to Myth*. London and Princeton.

Index

acclamation, 56f.

Achilles, 4f., 28

acta diurna, 73, 144

actors 107-9, 111, 145

Aeneas, 4, 46, 59

Aeschylus, tragic dramatist, 86, 91

Agrippa, M. Vipsanius, commander and statesman, 53, 60f.

Agrippina the Elder, devoted widow, 125f.

Alcibiades, politician and general, 17-24, 82, 110, 144, 146

Alexander of Abonuteichos, religious virtuoso, 98-100, 103

Alexander Romance, 36

Alexander the Great, 8, ch. 2 *passim*, 50, 53, 55, 77f., 83f., 91f., 110, 144

Antinoüs, favourite of the Emperor Hadrian, 146

Antony, Mark, triumvir, 48f., 55, 57, 59, 134f., 141

Apelles, painter, 29, 36, 89, 121

Appian, historian, 50

applause, 56f.

Archelaus of Macedon, patron of the arts, 83, 86, 143

Archias, Aulus Licinius, poet, 86f.

Archidice, courtesan, 119f.

Arignotus, lyre player, 110

Arion, poet, 85

Aristides the Just, politician and general, 17

Aristodemus, actor, 108f.

Aristophanes, comic dramatist, 18, 81f., 86, 110

Arsinoë II of Egypt, 122f., 128

Asclepiades, Marcus Aurelius, pancratiast, 71

Aspasia, courtesan, 120f., 145

Athenaeus, miscellanist, 121, 128

Augustus, emperor, 9, 35f., 49, ch. 4 *passim*, 92, 124, 133-6, 144

Bacchylides, composer of victory odes, 68

Bassilla, mime artiste, 112

Bathyllus, pantomime artist, 113

Brando, Marlon, 2

Caesar, Julius, general and statesman, 36, ch. 3 *passim*, 55f., 124, 132-4, 144

Callias, patron of sophists, 80

Callisthenes, historian, 31, 36

Calpurnia, wife of Julius Caesar, 124, 133

Calpurnianus, P. Aelius Gutta, charioteer, 74

Cato the Censor, politician, 84, 91

Catullus, poet, 119

chariot-racing, 72-6

Choerilus of Iasos, epic poet, 32

Choerilus of Samos, epic poet, 23, 143

Index

Cicero, orator and politician, 5, 91, 111

Cimon, politician, 15-17

Circus Maximus, 73

City Dionysia, 107

Claudian, composer of panegyrics, 87

Claudius, emperor, 126, 129

Clearchus of Heraclea, tyrant, 23

Cleomedes of Astypaleia, disgraced Olympic victor, 78

Cleopatra VII of Egypt, 55, 59, 131-6, 140f.

Colosseum, 114

Colossus of Rhodes, 55

Commodus, emperor and gladiator, 64, 113, 115

Conon, general, 16

Cornelia, exemplary Roman mother and widow, 123f., 128f.

Coroebus, athlete, 67

courtesans, see hetaerae

Curtius Rufus, Q., historian, 36

Cynisca of Sparta, owner of victorious chariot team, 72

deification, 22, 33, 48, 60f.

Democedes of Croton, physician, 68f., 84, 145

Diagoras of Rhodes, boxer, 70, 77

Diana, Princess of Wales, 2, 11, 49

Dio Cassius, historian, 47

Diocles, C. Apuleius, charioteer, 73f.

Diocletian, emperor, 49, 53

Diodorus, historian, 33, 77

Diogenes Laertius, biographer, 90, 144

Diogenes the Cynic, philosopher, 83, 146

Dionysus, 31, 85, 94

Dionysus, artists of, 109

divine honours, see deification

Domitian, emperor, 63f., 145

Dorieus, all-in wrestler, 69

epinikion, see victory ode

Euius of Chalcis, pipe-player, 110

Euripides, tragic dramatist, 86, 92, 94, 143

Exainetus of Acragas, foot-race victor, 72

Fabius Maximus Cunctator, Q., general, 46

fans, 7, 73, 75, 106, 108, 111-13, 145

Frontinus, writer on technical and military matters, 116

Fronto, M. Cornelius, orator and correspondent, 58, 91

Galen, physician, 77, 84

Garrick, David, actor, 3

Germanicus, general, 62, 126

Gilgamesh, king of Uruk, 4f.

gladiatorial contests, 42, 56

gladiators, 113-16

Glaucus of Carystus, boxer, 71

Gorgias of Leontini, sophist, 80f., 90

Hadrian, emperor, 24, 29, 49, 55

Hadrian of Tyre, sophist, 89f.

Halityrus, mime, 112

Harrison, George, 2

Helena, mother of Constantine the Great, 136

Hermerus, gladiator, 114

Herodotus, historian, 68, 85f., 92, 119

Herostratus, arsonist, 8

Hesiod, poet, 79, 106

hetaerae, 119f., 128

Hieron of Acragas, tyrant, 70